$ 11.95

Jerzy Kosinski

Twayne's United States Authors Series

Warren French, Editor

Indiana University

TUSAS 419

JERZY KOSINSKI
photo by Scientia © 1979

Jerzy Kosinski

By Norman Lavers

Arkansas State University

Twayne Publishers • Boston

Jerzy Kosinski

Norman Lavers

Copyright © 1982 by G. K. Hall & Company
Published by Twayne Publishers
A Division of G. K. Hall & Company
70 Lincoln Street
Boston, Massachusetts 02111

Book Production by Marne B. Sultz

Book Design by Barbara Anderson

Printed on permanent/durable acid-free
paper and bound in the United States of
America.

**Library of Congress Cataloging in
Publication Data**

Lavers, Norman.
    Jerzy Kosinski.

    (Twayne's United States authors series :
    TUSAS 419)
    Bibliography: p. 169
    Includes index.
    1. Kosinski, Jerzy, 1933–
—Criticism and interpretation.
I. Title. II. Series. 823
PS3561.08Z75   813'.54   81-7045
ISBN 0-8057-7352-5   AACR2

For Cheryl and Gawain

Contents

About the Author

Norman Lavers received the B.A. and M.A. degrees at San Francisco State College and the Ph.D. from the University of Iowa, where he was a member of the Iowa Writers Workshop. He has taught literature and creative writing at Northern Illinois University, Western Washington State College and Arkansas State University, where he now directs the writing program. His short stories and critical articles are widely published. His books include *Selected Short Stories* (1979) and the novel *Northwest Passage* (1982). His study of novelist Mark Harris was published in Twayne's U.S. Authors Series in 1978.

Preface

Jerzy Kosinski is a phenomenon. Who is there in America who has not heard something about his astonishing life?—the abandoned six-year-old child in Eastern Poland escaping Nazi extermination and hostile peasant harassment; the brilliantly engineered escape to the West from Soviet-dominated Eastern Europe; his arrival, penniless, in America with almost no English, followed two years later by the first of several best-selling books in his new language; the missing by one day being murdered by the Manson gang in Sharon Tate's house. The story goes on and on, and all his life has gone into his novels.

There are two questions I have had to deal with explicitly or implicitly throughout the course of the present book: is Kosinski, as some critics and reviewers have felt, not writing novels at all, but only records of his extraordinary life? Or is he actually, as he claims, refashioning these personal materials into serious unified works of literary art? And the second question: is a writer who has been so commercially successful (at last report, over 60 million novels sold), and who deals with such standard subjects of the crassest commercial fiction—secret agents, graphic sex and violence, current news events—merely exploiting his life and times for money, or does he have a serious vision to transmit to his readers?

I must confess that at the inception of my study, previously only having read his books casually over a period of years, I was uneasy about the answers I would find. By the time I had got only a little way into my study, however, it became obvious to me that the novels—making use of autobiography in numerous and complex ways—were nonetheless novels in every sense of the word, careful in craft, rich in invention, and serious in theme. As to the second question, of whether he is a serious writer worthy of serious critical attention: I would not have begun my study had I not been convinced he was a first-rate writer. But I have had to modify my first assessment. I am now convinced that Jerzy Kosinski is not merely a first-rate writer. Rather, he is a major writer of international stature, a philosophical writer in the tradition of Sartre and Camus—except a much better and more original novelist than either of these. These are, I know, bold statements. The purpose of my book is to demonstrate that they are not exaggerated.

In the first chapter I try, as nearly as I can, to give an account of what we know about the particulars of Kosinski's incredible life, so that we can compare them with the similar-appearing events that occur throughout his fiction. I also try to say something about the man, Kosinski, and about his beliefs, lifestyle, and aesthetic.

In the second chapter I discuss his first two, nonfiction, books, sociological studies of collective life in Russia. A surprising finding of the chapter is that these two works are very nearly proto-novels themselves, demonstrating the structure, the style, the themes, the very characters, that would occur in the later novels.

Chapter 3 deals in great detail with all the many themes of *The Painted Bird.* It is Kosinski's greatest work. The first three chapters of my book—his life, his nonfiction works, and *The Painted Bird*—form an essential foundation for fully understanding his later works, and I recommend that even a reader whose interest is only in one of the later novels read these three chapters as well as the later chapter dealing with the novel of his interest.

Chapters 4 through 8 deal, in chronological order, with Kosinski's next six novels. The last three of these chapters, in particular, form a unit, treating *Cockpit, Blind Date,* and *Passion Play,* which I see to be closely linked. Especially in these three novels, a steady transition can be seen. The protagonists become less egoistic, less revenge-prone, more human, more vulnerable. Both humor and sentiment appear almost for the first time in Kosinski's fiction. Structure becomes slightly more conventional, and for the first time, the possibility for love is present. These novels begin working out explicitly Kosinski's Existential philosophy of life, influenced by Heidegger and Jacques Monod, but also growing naturally out of Kosinski's own extreme experiences.

In Chapter 9 I give my final assessment of Jerzy Kosinski as an important twentieth-century world novelist.

I should point out an unusual, perhaps unique feature of this book. I was in correspondence with Kosinski throughout the writing of it. He was immensely valuable, of course, in the biographical section, where he helped me to eliminate some of the myths that have come to be reproduced in the many published accounts of his life. But that is not what I refer to here. It is Kosinski's own often expressed belief that once a novel is in print, the author becomes merely one more reader of it, his interpretations not necessarily better or worse than any other reader's. Therefore, when his readings of the novels on occasion differed from mine, he very scrupulously avoided forcing his opinions on me. Still, he could not always refrain—when we varied widely—from at least explaining to me what his intentions had been. Once or twice he convinced me I had misread him, and I silently and gratefully mended my error. But on other occasions where we continued to differ, though I still felt my readings were best, I thought his comments too valuable to lose, and so I have printed them alongside mine, either in the text or in footnotes. They not only provide an alternative reading, but give us special insights into the complex way he uses metaphor, and the way he builds a scene. The final effect is of a running dialogue between us as we discuss the novels. My book is immeasurably enriched by his contribution.

Norman Lavers

Arkansas State University

Acknowledgments

I would like to thank Kent H. Dixon for first stirring my interest in Jerzy Kosinski back in 1967.

Jerzy Kosinski himself was helpful at all stages in the production of this book, from sending me difficult to get articles, to easing the obtaining of permissions to quote various works. See Preface for an explanation of his more direct contributions to the book.

I would like to thank the Faculty Research Committee of Arkansas State University for a summer research grant that gave me valuable free time for research at the beginning of my study.

I also want to thank the following for permission to quote from certain material:

St. Martin's Press, Inc., for permission to quote from Jerzy Kosinski, *Passion Play,* St. Martin's Press, Inc.

Houghton Mifflin Co., for permisson to quote from Jerzy Kosinski, *Cockpit,* Houghton Mifflin Co.; Jerzy Kosinski, *Blind Date,* Houghton Mifflin Co.; and Jerzy Kosinski, *The Painted Bird,* Houghton Mifflin Co. Copyright © 1965, by Jerzy N. Kosinski.

Harcourt Brace Jovanovich, Inc., for permission to quote from Jerzy Kosinsky, *The Devil Tree,* Harcourt Brace Jovanovich, Inc.

Random House, Inc., for permisson to quote from *Steps,* by Jerzy N. Kosinski. Copyright © 1968 by Jerzy N. Kosinski. Reprinted by permission of Random House, Inc.

Viking Penguin Inc. for permisson to quote from material excerpted from *Writers at Work, The Paris Review Interviews* (Interview with Jerzy Kosinski) Fifth Series. Copyright © 1981 by The Paris Review, Inc. Reprinted by permisson of Viking Penguin Inc.

Gail Sheehy, for permission to quote from "The Psychological Novelist as Portable Man." Copyright © 1977 by Gail Sheehy.

Chronology

1933   Jerzy Nikodem Kosinski born June 14, Lodz, Poland, the only child of Mieczyslaw and Elzbieta (Liniecka) Kosinski.

1939–1945   Separated from his parents, who assume him dead. Wanders from village to village in Eastern Poland.

1942   Loses his speech in a traumatic accident.

1945   Found by his parents in an orphanage in Lodz.

1948   Regains his speech in hospital after serious skiing accident.

1950–1956   Ski instructor during winters in Zakopane, Poland; social instructor during summers (until 1956) in Miedzyzdroje on Baltic Ocean.

1953   M.A. in Political Science, University of Lodz.

1955   M.A. in History, University of Lodz.

1955–1957   Associate Professor, State Grantee, and Ph.D. candidate at Institute of Sociology and Cultural History, Polish Academy of Science, Warsaw. Research Assistant at Polish Academy of Arts and Science, and at Lomonosov University in Russia. During this period publishes two monographs on revolutionary movements of the nineteenth century; also exhibits his photographs in major international salons of photography, winning numerous awards.

1957   Comes to United States, December 20, with $2.80 in his pocket, and rudimentary knowledge of English; by March, speaks English fluently.

1958–1960   As Ford Foundation Fellow, does doctoral work at Columbia University in sociology of literary forms and language.

1960   *The Future Is Ours, Comrade* (written under the pseudonym Joseph Novak). Meets Mary Hayward Weir, widow of industrialist Ernest Weir, in New York.

1962   *No Third Path* (pseudonym, Joseph Novak). Marries Mary Hayward Weir, January 11.

1965   *The Painted Bird; Notes of the Author.* Becomes U.S. citizen.

1966   Best Foreign Book Award, France, for *The Painted Bird.*

1967   Guggenheim Fellow in Literature.

1968   *Steps; The Art of the Self.* Mary Weir dies of a brain tumor.

1968–1969   Fellow, Center for Advanced Studies, Wesleyan University.

1969   National Book Award for *Steps.* A baggage mix-up delays his flight to the home of Sharon Tate, where he was expected on August 7, the night of the Manson murders.

1969–1970   Senior Fellow, Council of Humanities, Princeton University.

1970   Award in Literature, National Institute of Arts and Letters and American Academy of Arts and Letters.

1970–1973   Visiting Professor of English Prose, School of Drama, Yale University; Resident Fellow, Davenport College, Yale University.

1971   *Being There.*

1973   *The Devil Tree.*

1973–1975   President of the American Center of P.E.N.; reelected 1974, serving the maximum two terms allowed.

1974   Brith Sholom Humanitarian Freedom Award.

1975   *Cockpit.* P.E.N. Resolution honoring Jerzy Kosinski for his contribution as president.

1977   *Blind Date.*

1978   Writes the screenplay for *Being There*. The American Civil Liberties Union Award.

1979   *Passion Play*. Film version of *Being There*, starring Peter Sellers, released with great success. Screenplay wins Writers Guild of America Best Screenplay Award.

1980   Polonia Media Perspectives Achievement Award.

1981   *The Devil Tree* (rev. ed.). Screenplay of *Being There* wins British Academy of Film and Television Arts (BAFTA) Best Screenplay of the Year Award.

Chapter One

"Larvatus Prodeo": Kosinski's Life and His Fiction

It is sometimes claimed that the novelist who has led the most adventurous and romantic life has an advantage over the sedentary writer whose study window overlooks the tranquil town where he was born. This, of course, is demonstrably not true. To take the usual examples, Joseph Conrad's life as sea captain to exotic ports, as gunrunner and lover of princesses, gave him grist for many tales, no doubt, but Jane Austen saw as far and as deeply in her native Hampshire, and who would call her an inferior novelist because her experience began and ended in a quiet English backwater?

Nevertheless we feel in our heart of hearts the adventurer, the escaper from death, the lover of beautiful women, has a headstart as novelist over the rest of us. Obviously, merely having the experience is not enough. The writer must then have the artistry to convert his experience into meaningful fiction. After all, countless children suffered as much or more than Kosinski during the Second World War, but only he wrote *The Painted Bird*. But a special advantage does come to Kosinski. *The Painted Bird* would be a powerful novel even had it been entirely invented. But because the reader knows its horrific details are based on horrific fact, the novel gains a difficult to calculate but no less real increment in power and resonance.

Ironically, however, there is a disadvantage for such a novelist: we can become more interested in his life than in his art, or, a more subtle danger, we can confuse the two. Aristotle has told us that poetry is superior to history because poetry (he meant any creative writing) gives us the universal, while history only tells us the local. To read all of Kosinski's novels as thinly disguised autobiography is to ignore Kosinski as artist, as creator. Furthermore, it can lead us to serious misreadings of his novels, making us, for instance, think Kosinski approves of all of his autobiographical-seeming protagonists, when in fact he is often being critical of them. Therefore my intention in the present chapter will be to put together as full a story of Kosinski's life as I can (based chiefly on Kosinski's own numerous recorded descriptions of his life), so that in following chapters I can begin outlining how he has used and transformed these materials to compose his fictions. No doubt most novelists have regularly ransacked their personal experiences for material for their novels; and many novels, perhaps, are indeed little more than novelized autobiography. But in few other novelists' work that I know is the subtle interplay between art and life so constant and conscious as in Kosinski's. This is true not just of his first novel, *The Painted Bird,* which draws heavily on his experiences as a child, but of the later, and in fact of the very latest novels, which, as he points out, are in certain ways even more autobiographical. The theme of the intricate relationship between life and art, between memory and creation, is so pervasive in his writing that, even after discussing it in the present chapter, I will have to keep coming back to it in the chapters where I discuss his individual novels.

His motto, we are told,[1] is *Larvatus Prodeo:* "I go forth disguised." It is an appropriate motto for his novels as well, for in them Kosinski sends forth his own life, his own experience, but "disguised"—and the disguise is the transmutation, the sublimation, the sea-change ("those are pearls, that were his eyes"[2]), of art.

Kosinski as "Painted Bird"

In Kosinski's first novel, *The Painted Bird,* a character captures a bird, and paints it in bright colors, perhaps, in a way, beautifying it. But when he releases it, and it tries to rejoin its fellows, they fall on it and peck it to death. The drab brown birds cannot accept the gaudy stranger in their midst.[3]

The painted bird stands as a metaphor for the little boy who is the protagonist of that novel, but it can stand as well for Kosinski himself, who, with his hawk nose and penetrating eyes, has always been the odd bird, the misfit, the outcast, the dark-eyed, dark-haired Jew in a blond, blue-eyed, Gentile culture, the individualist in a collective society, the mute, the foreigner, the "inner emigré" in his own country—and finally, of course, the artist, the idealist, in a world of practical, nine-to-five materialism.

Jerzy Kosinski—the first name is pronounced Yahr-zhuh, but he will accept almost any pronunciaton except Jerry[4]—was born in 1933 in Lodz, Poland. His parents were educated and well-to-do. His mother was a pianist of professional caliber, though she seldom performed in public. His father was a philologist, a student of languages, by profession, who after early retirement, worked as a freelance linguistic consultant and expert in international industrial norms. Both, perhaps, were disappointed people, born at the wrong moment in history. His father's whole life was devoted to flight, physical and spiritual: "He was born in Russia," Kosinski tells us. "He saw the Revolution of 1905, then World War I, then he escaped from Russia during the Bolshivik Revolution, and then he lived through the Second World War. So if anyone had a reason to be fed up, he had. And he withdrew from the twentieth century altogether. He studied Ancient Greece, and the origins of the European languages. It was his escape device."[5]

Two months after the German invasion of Poland in 1939 (Kosinski was six years old) he became separated from his parents, who assumed him dead. The next years he wandered throughout villages of Polesie and Volhynia in Eastern Europe—his dark coloring contrasting suspiciously with that of the blond peasants—believing himself to be either a gypsy or a Jew.[6] The Germans were rounding up gypsies and Jews to send to the death camps to be gassed and incinerated (the death trains passing through the landscape provide a somber motif to *The Painted Bird*). The penalty for harboring gypsy or Jew was severe, and so the peasants did not welcome the wandering child. As a potentially dangerous outcast, he was often treated cruelly, threatened, abused, at times narrowly escaping death. The psychic pressure was so extreme that when he was nine, he lost his speech in an accident, and from then on, to his other disadvantages in that society was added his inability to communicate verbally.[7]

In 1945, at the termination of the war, he was found by his parents in an orphanage, still mute, and half crazed. For the next two years, he went to the school for the handicapped and YMCA rehabilitation center. He slept by day in his clothes, and at night wandered the streets, perhaps craving the freedom of his days wandering the villages. As therapy, they took him to the Karkonosze mountains where an old ski guide taught him skiing. He became an enthusiastic skier. Then at fourteen he had a serious skiing accident, and during his recovery in the hospital, he suddenly regained his speech. With his father and YMCA staff as tutors, he worked his way through high school in one year.[8] He then went to the University of Lodz, where he took the M.A. in History (1953) and in Political Science (1955). Both his dissertations were, ironically, devoted to the tragic plight of political opposition in nineteenth-century Russia, and he continued the study under the auspices of the Polish Academy of Sciences, at Lomonosov University in the USSR, and the Polish Academy of Sciences in Warsaw.[9]

Kosinski's academic excellence was noticed and encouraged, but all was not well. Russia, under the Soviets, and Poland to a somewhat lesser extent, were collectivized societies. Students formed groups which met at regular intervals for the purpose of public self-criticism, or criticism of one's fellows. The individual personality was seen as an impediment to full socialization, to be expunged at all costs.

The contrast with Kosinski's early life of deprivation and suffering—but of absolute freedom and independence—could not have been more extreme. For a strong individualist like Kosinski, collective life was insupportable. He used every ploy he could think of to avoid a possibly fatal confrontation with it. But even so, his rights as a student were twice suspended, and he was threatened with "resettlement"—the euphemism for being sent to a forced-labor camp.[10]

Feeling a need for artistic expression (writing would have been impossible under the regime), he enrolled in night-school classes in photography. In a short time he became a prize-winning photographer. Photography, which ostensibly merely records "what is there," is, therefore—at least as compared to a novel—devoid of the subjectivity of the author. If someone objected that his photographs were critical of the society, he could easily turn the charge against them, saying he had only photographed what was in front of him and that it was *they* who were judging the scene critically. Photography, then, was the only means of expression open in a totalitarian state, and even with photography Kosinski could get himself into trouble—some of the pictures he took of undraped females suggested creeping Western decadence![11]

"The photographic darkroom emerged as a perfect metaphor for my life. . . . It became a kind of temple." The darkroom was the single place in the collectivist society that could be legitimately locked. Once the red light went on outside the door, no one would dare enter for fear of destroying the light-sensitive photographic materials. The very packets of photographic paper could not be opened, and therefore were ideal to conceal things in. Kosinski not only sneaked moments of privacy in the darkroom, but also brought in forbidden books—by Dostoevski, for instance—to read there.[12]

"When I was growing up in a Stalinist society my guidelines were: Am I going to survive physically? Am I going to survive as a sane being? Since I was in conflict with the society, my real plight had to remain hidden. I avoided having close friends who would know too much about me, and could be used against me. Until I left for America I lived the life of an 'inner emigré,' as I called myself."[13]

In the USSR, where he was pursuing his doctoral studies, he finally became convinced that if he remained in a Communist country his fate would be sealed: he was philosophically and morally opposed to communism and, as such, was faced with a lifetime in labor camps or prison. He decided to escape.

The moment was auspicious. He used the creaking bureaucracy and the confusion of the aftermath of the Hungarian revolution, and Khrushchev's bent for liberalism, to obtain a passport. He even invented several high-up bureaucrats and sponsors, and, writing their letters on the official stationery he himself printed, corresponded with high Party and Police officials until they issued his passport and let him buy an air ticket to the United States in local currency. These letters might be considered his first—and demonstrably his most effective— pieces of fiction. Once abroad, he meant to defect and make a new life in the country he entered. He wanted to move to a "large, multiethnic giant where I could be altogether left alone." Because he knew Latin and French, he thought he could most quickly adapt in a Romance-language-speaking country. Therefore, starting, as he claims, at the beginning of the alphabet, he applied to Argentina and Brazil for visas. Ironically, both turned him down because of his Marxist background. Then, he says, he went to the other end of the alphabet, applied to the United States, and was granted entrance as a "highly skilled alien."[14]

America on $2.80

Kosinski's novels are often picaresque in structure and action, which is to say, they are fragmented into short episodes, and marked by extreme and sudden changes—from rags to riches, from safety to danger, wandering from country to country, through every walk of society. Kosinski's own life exactly resembles such a picaresque novel. On December 20, 1957, twenty-four years old, $2.80 in his pocket, and with rudimentary knowledge of English, he entered the United States.[15]

In the next few months he had an assortment of jobs, anything he could get—paint scraper, chauffeur, truck driver—in the meantime memorizng lists of words out of dictionaries, seeing the same movie over and over, reading Russian classics word by word with both the Russian and English before him, until in four months he was fluent in English.[16] He had pretended to his own government that he had a grant to study in the United States; and now he actually got one, a Ford Foundation grant to pursue doctoral work at Columbia.

He was presenting a report, in one of his classes, on Russian collectivization, when one of his classmates, who happened to be an editor at Doubleday, encouraged him to write a book on the subject. He did, and the book (*The Future Is Ours, Comrade*, published under the pseudonym Joseph Novak) was serialized by *The Saturday Evening Post*, condensed by *Reader's Digest*, and quickly became a best seller. From the $2.80 he had begun with, he now had $150,000 in the bank.

Marriage and High Life

Mary Weir, widow of steel magnate Ernest Weir, read the book, was impressed by it and wrote to Kosinski. They became acquainted and soon were married. The mute and homeless orphan of nine, the impoverished and deracinated immigrant of twenty-four, at twenty-nine was living a life of unimaginable luxury aboard vast yachts, private jets, and in any of numerous villas in America and Europe. "I had lived the American nightmare, now I was living the American dream." The only contribution he could afford to make in this new style of life was to pay the tips wherever they went. It will be sufficient comment on the level of the life to say that the tipping completely exhausted the considerable sum of money he had made from his first books.

But then Mary Weir Kosinski died of a brain tumor. The wealth, left to her in trust, went back to the Weir estate, and Kosinski was once more an ordinary citizen. But not quite. In the meantime he had published *The Painted Bird,* which made him a celebrated novelist. He had tipped away even the money made from that successful novel, so to support himself he got jobs teaching at Wesleyan, Princeton, and Yale. The novels continued to appear, and now he writes full time, lives mainly in a sparsely furnished Manhattan apartment, but travels, for several months of the year, through North and South America and Europe, lying on sunny beaches, or following his old interest, skiing, or his new interest, playing polo.[17]

But the picaresque career is one of violence and sudden death, as well, and that element has not left his life. In 1969, a baggage mix-up delayed his flight to the home of his close friends Sharon Tate and Roman Polanski. He was furious—until he found out that on the night he was scheduled to be there, the Manson group had murdered everyone in the house.[18]

Autobiography and Fiction

The question I began with—and the reason I have detailed these events in Kosinski's life—is the extent to which Kosinski's autobiography interpenetrates his fiction. Anyone who has read very much of his fiction will have found nearly everything I have recounted here occurring in one or other of his novels, and certain of the events recurring in more than one novel. And yet the question is surprisingly subtle and complex. As I say, I will need to come back to it with each of his novels as I discuss them in detail in the following chapters.

When Kosinski himself is asked to comment on the degree to which his novels are autobiographical, his answers do not always seem consistent. When critics claim that his works are autobiographical, he indignantly insists that they are *novels,* artistically created works of the imagination. When critics say his works are *not* autobiographical, however, he just as indignantly insists that every word in them is true. He says, for instance, that when he was writing *The Painted Bird* his wife "learned of my past through my writing."[19] "All my writing is autobiographical, *all,*" he told a Literary Guild interviewer.[20] "Every incident [in *The Painted Bird*] is true,"[21] he has said.

But when George Plimpton and Rocco Landesman interviewed him for the *Paris Review,* he addressed the question much more subtly. Interviewer: Given the unusual circumstances of your life, many people think of your work—the first two novels, anyway—as nonfiction." Kosinski: "Well, to say that *The Painted Bird,* for example, is nonfiction, or even autobiographical, may be convenient for classification, but it's not easily justified. What we remember lacks the hard edge of fact. To help us along we create little fictions, highly subtle and individual scenarios which clarify and shape our experience. The remembered event becomes a fiction, a structure made to accommodate certain feelings. This is obvious to me. If it weren't for these structures, art would be too personal for the artist to create, much less for the audience to grasp."[22]

Kosinski is saying that even if our intention is to write straight autobiography, we must write chiefly from memory, and memory itself fictionalizes our experience, because memory is an editing device: we remember what was subjectively most important to us and forget much else, and we remember in a certain form and sequence in order to organize in our minds what our experience was. And when we write down these memories, they are further distanced, by being put in the conventional form of writing, and ordered on the page in such a way that we can write them coherently and our audience can read them.

But Kosinski has never described straight autobiography as his purpose for writing. "The essential stage of . . . writing . . .," he says, "is the process whereby the writer comes to stand outside the experience he intends to mirror in his book. The chief element of this 'alienation' is the conscious desire to examine oneself and the experience from 'without,' from a standpoint at which both the writer himself and his surroundings lose their concrete features, and separate themselves from everyday reality . . . . Between external reality and his own imagination the writer constructs one curtain after another . . . . These curtains cannot completely veil reality; they merely obscure its patterns . . . . As an actor playing Hamlet is neither Hamlet nor merely an actor, but, rather, an actor as Hamlet, so is a fictive event neither an actual event nor totally a created fiction with no base in experience; *it is an event as fiction.*"[23]

Explaining this passage to me, Kosinski has said that if we consider Kosinski as Hamlet (in other words, as the subject of the work) and his fictional protagonist as the actor (the one who portrays Kosinski's life), then we find that the fictional protagonist is not absolutely free in his actions, nor are the actions absolutely autobiographical, taking place, rather, in the space between the autobiographical event and the fictional protagonist. Kosinski therefore can write of the actual event, but it is "an event as fiction."

Kosinski's Language and Attitudes toward Language

What inevitably first occurs to us when we come to discuss Kosinski's language is that he has chosen to write in his third or fourth language, a language he only had a rudimentary knowledge of two years before he wrote his first book in English.

What cannot help next occurring to us is that Kosinski is thereby in an illustrious tradition of polylingual Slavic expatriates who have elected to write in English, the tradition of Joseph Conrad and Vladimir Nabokov. Let us compare and contrast them for a moment.

Joseph Conrad was born a Pole, knew Russian, emigrated to France, and learned French; then, in his early twenties he moved to England and learned English. By all accounts he spoke English with an atrocious accent, and much preferred to speak French (as he did when he was with his friend Henry James). Nevertheless, when he settled down to become a novelist, it was English he chose to write in, and his written English is rich and aureate, vast in vocabulary, intricate in rhythm and syntax.

Vladimir Nabokov was fluent in four languages, English, French, German, and his native Russian. He claimed that English was actually his first literary language, since as a child he had for a time an English nurse who read to him in that language. But he wrote and published in Russian and French, before he finally established his reputation writing in English. Once more, like Conrad, his written English is rich and golden, intricate and allusive, and his vocabulary spans several disciplines, from etymology to entomology. But, to judge by recordings of his voice I have heard, he spoke English with an accent and a distinctly foreign intonation.

Kosinski, born and educated in Poland, of Polish, though Russian-educated parents who spoke Russian at home (and Kosinski and his philologist father spoke Latin to each other over the telephone in order to foil the official censors[24]), learned some French, before finally learning English in his early twenties. I have spoken to Kosinski over the telephone. He speaks at tremendous speed, his wit has almost a professional comedian's rhythm and timing, and he speaks with very little accent, though certainly with a non-native lilt. (He has been a very effective, entertaining guest on the "Tonight" show on many occasions.) So I think it is fair to say he speaks English much better than Conrad or Nabokov. He writes much differently, however, for as they are rich and ample, ironically, he is stripped and "plain-style." "I used to count words the way Western Union does; my prose was like a night letter. Every word was there for a reason, and if not, I would cross it out. . . . I wanted to make the language of my fiction as unobtrusive as possible, almost transparent, so that the reader would be drawn right away into each dramatic incident. I suppress in my prose any language which calls attention to itself. . . . It is the opposite, for instance, of what Nabokov does. His language is made visible . . . like a veil or a transparent curtain with a beautiful design. You cannot help seeing the curtain as you peek into the intimate room behind. My aim, though, is to remove the veil."[25]

I think this is certainly the method, and the effect, of Kosinski's writing at its best. It is the power of the event and the cumulative impact of the actions that create the effects in Kosinski's novels, not the richness of language. The language does what is necessary, then gets out of the way.

On the other hand, I do not wish to overstate the plainness or neutrality of the language. When it is consciously examined by the reader, he will find it absolutely accurate in diction, and surprisingly rich in images, but images which push the reader always toward visualizing the scene before him. Nor is the language monolithic. It is constantly shifting in subtle ways to serve best the particular scene at hand, and quite different styles and vocabularies are used from novel to novel.

The disadvantages of writing in a language other than that which one has grown up with are obvious. "The main [disadvantage] for me," admits Kosinski, "is that I am never certain whether my English prose is sufficiently clear. Also, I rarely allow myself to use English in a truly spontaneous way and therefore, I always have a sense of trembling."[26] He has often told the story of how he used telephone operators to help him with his writing. "Late at night you have no one to ask. I would

dial the telephone operator . . . I got incredible advice. I did it
hundreds of times—I still do it."[27]

But Kosinski has found as well special advantages in writing in an
adopted tongue: "English helped me sever myself from my childhood,
from my adolescence. In English I don't make involuntary associations
with my childhood."[28] We might be moved to ask why a writer should
want to be "severed" from the associations of his childhood. The answer
is evidently complex. First of all we should remember that his childhood was traumatic. And as to his adolescence, he has said, rather
enigmatically, "I did not like myself in Poland."[29]

But if he wanted to be separated from his past, it was not in order to
put it out of his mind, but rather, to have sufficient detachment to be
able to write about it. "I abandoned my maternal language upon
quitting my country. . . . English still being new for me, I can write
without passion, freed from emotional outbursts connected with my
native tongue."[30] Also, "I could never write fiction, for instance, in
Polish or Russian because I was suppressed by the linguistic tradition,
suppressed by the grammar."[31]

Gail Sheehy, interviewing Kosinski for *Psychology Today,* asked him,

"When after you came to America and began writing in English, did you feel
less, or more, articulate?" Kosinski: "It was a great surprise to me, one of
many surprises of my life, that when I began speaking English, I felt freer to
express myself, not just my views but my personal history, my quite private
drives, all the thoughts that I would have found difficult to reveal in my
mother tongue. It seemed that the languages of my childhood and
adolescence—Polish and Russian—carried a sort of mental suppression. By
the time I was 25, in America, my infancy in English had ended and I
discovered that English, my stepmother tongue, offered me a sense of
revelation, of fulfillment, of abandonment—everything contrary to the
anxiety my mother tongue evoked. Come to think of it, there is something
ominous even in the phrase 'mother tongue.' I have talked with some of my
compatriots, writers, film makers, and other artists who in midlife emigrated from Eastern Europe and have been forced to embrace English,
French, or German as their second language. Like me, most of them profess
to be creatively freer in the adopted language."[32]

The freedom from his mother tongue, like his freedom from country,
from family—though all these freedoms were traumatically forced

upon him—have given him finally the freedom to go as far, and to go in whatever direction, his fictions demand: "I am alone. I have lost my family, my wife, my country. That is why I create freely, without worry. Even my friend Polanski cannot do as much. He has ties which do not permit him to go beyond a certain limit in cruelty."[33]

Kosinski's Aesthetic

Kosinski is so fluent and outspoken on his methods and purposes that I cannot do better in this section than to let him speak for himself:

"I have never considered literature to be as important as the public highway system, for instance. Reading fiction is an esoteric pursuit."[34]

"I think [the written word] will survive where it has always really been—at the edge of contemporary sensibility. I think that's the proper place for it anyhow. Reading novels has always been an experience limited to a very small percentage of the so-called public. . . . Today, people are absorbed in the most common denominator, the *visual*. It requires no education to watch TV. It knows no age limit. Your infant child can watch the same program you do. . . . Language requires some inner triggering; television doesn't. The image is ultimately accessible, i.e., extremely attractive. And, I think, ultimately deadly, because it turns the viewer into a bystander. . . . From way back, our major development as a race of frightened beings has been towards how to avoid facing the discomfort of our existence, primarily the possibility of an accident, immediate death, ugliness, and the ultimate departure In terms of all this, television is a very pleasing medium: one is always the observer. The life of discomfort is always accorded to others. . . . Literature does not have this ability to soothe. You have to evoke and by evoking, you yourself have to provide your own inner setting. When you read about a man who dies, part of you dies with him because you have to recreate his dying inside your head" (*PR*, 204–205).

Interviewer: "You say that literature demands more involvement and more effort from the reader than the visual media. Is this why your last two novels have been so spare?" Kosinski: "Yes. I do trust the reader. I think he is perfectly capable of filling in the blank spaces, of supplying what I purposefully withdrew. . . . He has to make the same decisions my protagonist is making. . . ." Interviewer: "Your intent, then, is subversive. You want to involve, to implicate the reader via his own imagination." Kosinski: "I guess I do. Once he is implicated he is an accomplice, he is provoked, he is involved, he is purged. That's why I won't give him moral guidelines. The reader must ask himself questions. Was it his curiosity that dragged him into the midst of my story, or was it recognition, his complicity? For me this is the ultimate purpose of writing" (*PR,* 206–207).

Interviewer: "Doesn't it bother you that there are so many different reactions and interpretations [of your novels]?" Kosinski: "No. How do we know what Camus wanted to say in his novels? We only know what we perceive and we read Camus for whatever we get from him now. A writer prompts a certain vision; he does not delineate it. His purpose is to awake, to trigger; the rest cannot be guessed. After all, if the writer's imagination is free enough to arrive at this triggering moment, why shouldn't the reader's imagination be equally good? A writer is not superior to anyone; he merely reflects a human ability to evoke" (*PR,* 202–203).

"An incident is simply a moment of life's drama of which we are aware as it takes place. This awareness and the intensity of it decides, in my view, whether our life is nothing but a barely perceived existence, or meaningful living. To intensify life, one must not only recognize each moment as an incident full of drama, but, above all, oneself as its chief protagonist. To bypass that moment, to dilute it in the gray everydayness, is to waste the most precious ingredient of living: the awareness of being alive. That's why in my fiction I stress an incident, as opposed, let's say, to a popular culture, which stresses a plot. Plot is an artificially imposed notion of preordained 'destiny' that usually dismisses the importance of life's each moment. Yet, that moment carries the essence of our life."[35]

Kosinski Himself

I have never seen Kosinski in person, but all descriptions of him stress his hawk nose, his dark penetrating eyes, and his slender build (5' 11", 132 pounds[36]), which is nonetheless wiry and strong from skiing, tennis and polo.

Through his own words and the words of interviewers and friends, two different pictures of his lifestyle emerge. The first suggests that he is as nervous, as mobile, as constantly prepared for disaster as the picaresque heroes, the secret agents, of his fiction. The introduction to a 1972 interview tells us, for instance, that Kosinski knows of twenty-five friendly places to write—or to hide—in Manhattan alone.[37] His apartment is described as sparse:

A compact living room-bedroom, a kitchenette, a bathroom, and, for photographic pursuits, a dressing room made into a darkroom. Small as it all is, however . . . it was still large enough for Mr. Kosinski to hide in.

Before saying good-by to Mr. Kosinski, we demanded a firsthand look at his disappearance act. Miss von Fraunhofer ushered us down the hall, while Mr. Kosinski hid. Then we came back. We looked everywhere very carefully—in the closets, under the sofa, behind every cabinet, even in the darkroom. There was no question, the author of *Being There* wasn't there. We gave up.

At that point, out came Mr. Kosinski. "Once," he told us, "I hid for a whole weekend. I came out only for food and work. People were in and out too, but they never found me."[38]

He is among friends. Yet once or twice a day he slips out to the driveway and half-buries himself in the trunk of his convertible. Pulling out a variety of items, he examines and rearranges them, handling each one with such reverence that one imagines the contents to be rare minerals or perhaps high explosives.

Upon closer scrutiny, the observer will note that the items are quite pedestrian; canned foods, a drop-legged bed, nonalcoholic beverages, notebooks to write in and novels to read, cash, weapons (or what the owner refers to as "relative protection systems," the "strength of character" being the only absolute one), and an odd-looking, charred, one-quart can with holes punched in its sides and a wire loop for a handle. This, the owner will explain, is an item essential to survival without human help; a comet.[39]

He remains a most secretive person:

Interviewer: "What do you do with the drafts [of your writings]?" Kosinski: "I put them away in a bank vault. I am secretive. I close things. I lock them. I have fifteen different places where my things are hidden. Some of the bank vaults where I send the drafts are almost bigger than my apartment. I am always afraid that some societal force will go after me, and will try to penetrate not only my apartment—let them do it!—but my inner life, which is reflected in my writing and in my letters."

Interviewer: "Do you ever think about abandoning writing altogether?" Kosinski: "I do. What if I found myself again in a police state? Or, to be more exact, what if a police state found me? I find it very telling that during the fourteen years of my existence in the U.S., I have always kept a photographic darkroom in my apartment. The darkroom remains even today my device for escape from the ideologies of political terror."

Interviewer: "Could you see yourself starting all over again—new country, new language?" Kosinski: "It's a nightmare, but I do think about it. Yes, I could."[40]

But from the descriptions of his friends, a different Kosinski emerges, one dedicated absolutely to his art, whose life, over the years, has become disciplined into regular habits to aid in the production of that art. Film director Milos Forman, for example, has said, "When trying to understand Kosinski some people concentrate too much on his personal history, others too much on his fiction. But what you must come to see is that Kosinski is a mixture of both. Both are very real to him."[41] Robert Geniesse, a longtime friend who first met Kosinski in 1958, was asked in 1979 how Kosinski had changed in the past two decades. "He hasn't changed. The only difference is that he is busier. I don't see him much now. The only thing that everyone forgets about Kosinski is how hard he works. He spends 95 per cent of his time writing. And writing is a solitary task. It seems as if he travels around a lot. But in his own fashion Jerzy has settled into a pattern: the apartment in New York [and for several years now, it has been at the same address] and in Switzerland; his skiing; his polo and his writing. In fact, at this point, with a novel out on the stands [*Passion Play*], I'm sure he's already deep into the next work."[42]

Chapter Two

Kosinski's Non-fiction Novels: *The Future Is Ours, Comrade,* and *No Third Path*

It is not, perhaps, generally realized that Kosinski's first two books in English were nonfiction sociological works dealing with collectivized life in the Soviet Union, published under the pen name of Joseph Novak. They are interesting and readable books, but would not concern us here in a study of Kosinski's fiction if it were not for the fact that in them we see in the earliest stages many of the methods and techniques of his fiction, the episodic structures, the stripped prose, the seemingly noncommittal reporting, the very characters, episodes, and metaphors of his later novels.

In 1953 the twenty-year-old Kosinski received the M.A. in Political Science from the University of Lodz in Poland, and in 1955 the M.A. in History. In 1956, as an associate professor of sociology in the Institute of Sociology and Cultural History, Polish Academy of Science, in Warsaw, he was able to visit the USSR several times to pursue research for his doctoral studies on the relationship between the individual and the collective (his superiors naturally expected that his studies would confirm the priority of the collectivity over the individual). It was while in Russia, traveling widely, relatively unrestricted, interviewing people, that he took notes that would eventually go into his two books on collective life in Russia.

When he entered the United States December 20, 1957, one of his first projects in systematically teaching himself his new language was to translate these notes into English. In July 1958 he got a Ford Foundation grant to work for a doctorate in political sociology at Columbia's New School for Social Research. He was giving a class presentation on collective life in Russia when one of his classmates, who happened to be an editor at Doubleday, suggested he write a book. That book is *The Future Is Ours, Comrade.*

It was serialized by *Saturday Evening Post* and condensed by *Reader's Digest.* The book was well received and Kosinski ended up making $150,000 from it. He also received thousands of admiring letters, from, among others, Konrad Adenauer, Bertrand Russell, and, as I have already mentioned, Mary Weir, whom he eventually married.

The Future Is Ours, Comrade

The book consists almost entirely of interviews with people from all walks of life, from all parts of the country. People fully in step with the regime, and people in desperate trouble because of their opposition to it. The interviews are arranged into chapters obviously intended to be representative of different professions or conditions. For instance, the first two chapters interview people about their living conditions. Kosinski visits an old-age home where the elderly have been left by their children to die, because the children simply have no room for the old people in their crowded houses. The young people wander the streets all night for the same reason—there is no room in their cramped and crowded apartments. People take pride in their city, in national buildings, in Lenin's tomb, as a substitute for taking pride in their homes. Chapter three deals with the Victorian morality thrust on the people; chapter four, attitudes toward work. Other chapters report interviews with people connected with hospitals, the military, politics, or deal with the Soviet Jews, attitudes toward the West, and other touchy subjects.

The Future Is Ours as Proto-Novel

"I realize that in my contacts with daily life in the U.S.S.R. I inevitably added my own subjectivity to the subjectivity of those describing their part in that life. In an effort to cut this down to a minimum, I was always glad to let other people talk and limited my role to listening and faithfully recording the conversations" (286).[1]

This is true up to a point. Kosinski has in the main let his characters speak for themselves. But he has, naturally, left to himself responsibility for selecting which interviews he put in his book and which he left out, and he has arranged them in the pattern that suited him. The pattern, the selections, offer as a cumulative effect an overwhelming indictment of Soviet collective society. It is shown to be utterly dehumanizing, a system to destroy or pervert whatever is natural and human and decent, to advance and elevate whatever is small and mean and mechanical or antlike in its total servitude to the state.

I am not doubting for a moment the accuracy or truthfulness of the effect, but am only suggesting that the effect has, to a certain extent, been achieved by Kosinski's careful editing and organizing of his notes. A person sympathetic to the Soviet regime might conceivably have taken the same raw material and selected and arranged it in such a way as to give an impression quite different from Kosinski's.

In short, Kosinski had a theme: the hatefulness of the collective society; and, far from trying to "cut [his subjectivity] down to a minimum," he organized his materials in such a way as to demonstrate the theme. To the extent that he did this, he was operating novelistically, rather than, as he claims, scientifically, or objectively. The final paragraph of the book, just like the final section in many of his novels, is a carefully designed metaphor meant to comment on all that has gone before it. The scene depicts Kosinski leaving the USSR: "The plane climbed higher. The steamy, curling clouds which hugged it tightly fell away. The sky contrasted sharply with the earth below, on which darkness had already fallen" (286). Surely this intends to show the Soviet collective shrouded in darkness, while man's individual spirit, disentangling itself from the murkiness, climbs toward the light of freedom.

My only point is that it seems to me that because of the novelistic methods Kosinski uses, the proto-novel he writes in *The Future Is Ours, Comrade* is very close in structure and technique to his actual novels and is indeed the testing ground for the novels he was already beginning to think about writing.[2]

The Kosinski Protagonist

"As a minor bureaucrat from one of the Satellite countries, enjoying the confidence of a number of highly situated U.S.S.R. officials who were responsible for my visit, I was invited to Russia for a protracted stay and allowed to arrange my Soviet life according to my own wishes, without being hampered or limited by anyone" (16).

This is extremely reminiscent of the typical Kosinski protagonist: from an outside society, critical of, yet somehow in the confidence of, highly placed officialdom, free of restraint, a free agent, able to act on his own, in a situation where everyone else is restrained. He is a lone agent on no one's side, the observer from outside, the individual where individuality is forbidden, privileged with freedom, yet because of his freedom condemned to be alone. We are reminded of Levanter, the protagonist of *Blind Date,* who calls himself a "small investor," or the double agent Tarden, in *Cockpit,* who finally is an agent only for his own freedom.

The Kosinski Structure

As I have said, the theme of *The Future Is Ours, Comrade* emerges powerfully, but it emerges as a result of the cumulative impact of dozens of finely etched vignettes. Each little story, each capsule life history, is one more piece in the emergent pattern. But no one scene is causally connected to the next. With few exceptions, characters do not know each other, do not recur in the book. Their only connection is that they appear before the ubiquitous Kosinski, tell their tale, and have it noted down. The incidents, the individual moments, are the more sharply seen because we know they are complete unto themselves. We are not waiting for them to lead to something else.

Clearly, this episodic, incident-centered patterning forms the structure of Kosinski's novels as well (though the most recent novels are showing some movement in the direction of "plot"). Let me quote Kosinski again on his rationale for this structure in his novels: "An incident is simply a moment of life's drama of which we are aware as it takes place. This awareness and the intensity of it decides, in my view, whether our life is nothing but a barely perceived existence, or meaningful living. . . . That's why in my fiction I stress an incident, as opposed, let's say, to a popular culture, which stresses a plot. Plot is an artificially imposed notion of preordained 'destiny' that usually dismisses the importance of life's each moment. Yet, that moment carries the essence of our life."[3]

Kosinski has, indeed, a number of aesthetic and philosophical reasons for preferring the incident over the plot, which I will touch on in later chapters. But here, at the beginning of his career, it is interesting to note that his professional training as a sociologist had some influence on what we see as the typical structure of his novels. The structure of the nonfiction books (which, I am saying, anticipates the structure of the novels) is necessarily fragmented because of the methodology of traveling about interviewing dozens of people and making the compilation of their interviews the body of the books. The decision to collect, through interviews, the opinions and attitudes of Soviet citizens about themselves and their environment is based, Kosinski tells me, on the social theory, growing out of the work of William I. Thomas, American sociologist (1863–1947), and Florian Znaniecki, his Polish-American collaborator (1882–1957) and a creator of his own system of sociology, that society is in the minds of individuals; that it is meaning that acts upon personality rather than objectively defined sets of social conditions. Also, that in its biographical dimension, personality enters into the constitution of the social system. These concepts helped to determine the structure of Kosinski's first books, and the concepts, and the structures, have persisted through the novels.

Character and Incident

Not only were the typical, superficially autobiographical protagonist and the episodic structure already present in Kosinski's first two nonfiction books, but indeed many characters and incidents and images appearing in the later novels make their first appearance here; and everywhere the handling, the tone, of the incidents is just what we find in the later novels.[4]

For example, an incident which has not (as yet) appeared in one of his novels but is characteristic of the incidents in his novels occurs in the third chapter (on sexual morality). Kosinski is attracted to a pretty girl, they see each other five or six times, she does her hair in a ponytail, lowers her blouse, narrows her skirts—in imitation of Western styles—and suddenly is punished, thrown out of the youth organization, threatened with expulsion from school, and allowed to "volunteer" herself to spend four months harvesting in a remote part of the USSR. He gets on the train and leaves. It is so much like an incident in one of his novels—his responsibility for her disaster, his own ability to leave it all behind—and the story so patly makes the point (about the Soviet's Victorian morality) he wants to make just then, that really all that differentiates the scene from a scene in one of his novels is our response to it: in this case we read it as fact; if it appeared in one of the novels, we would read it as fiction. If indeed Kosinski regularly uses incidents from his life in his fiction, he has already, in this nonfiction book, developed his particular technique for translating his experiences into writing.

In *No Third Path,* the second book Kosinski wrote from his notes, we see Gavrila, who appears to be identically the same Gavrila who rescues the boy in *The Painted Bird,* and becomes his political adviser;[5] we see in Demyon V., wheeler-dealer organizer of a Moscow Youth Festival (330–39), the first hint of Romarkin in *Blind Date;* and also in *No Third Path,* we meet that marvelous, almost Conradian character, the bookkeeper who feels himself to be "free as a bird" (52) because he has learned to hide out by sitting in the toilet stalls of the lavatories of large public buildings: "You enter, the entire room is so clean that it glitters, you lock the door behind you, and you are *alone.* Completely alone— have you ever thought of it? *No one* has the right to disturb you. You sit and think or read a newspaper if you like—no one cares, no one can intrude! This is, so to say, the *essence* of solitude, right? Around you is marble, shining floor, fluorescent light, ventilation. . . . You sit— like a Greek god!" (54). The business about using the toilets as a hiding place, a place of privacy, is used in the novel *Steps* (see note 8 to this chapter).

Most strikingly, the first mention of the "painted bird" theme is found in *No Third Path.* Varvara, an individualistic girl he meets, tells him:

"When I was a little girl . . . I wanted to learn all I could about the behavior of various animals. I remember how once a group of us kids caught a sparrow in a trap. He struggled with all his might—tiny heart thumping desperately—but I held on tight. We then painted him purple and I must admit he actually looked much better—more proud and unusual. After the paint had dried we let him go to rejoin the flock. We thought he would be admired for his beautiful and unusual coloring, become a model to all the gray sparrows in the vicinity, and they would make him their king. He rose high and was quickly surrounded by his companions. For a few moments their chirping grew much louder and then—a small object began plummeting earthward. We ran to the place where it fell. In a mud puddle lay our purple sparrow—dead. His blood mingled with the paint. . . . The water was rapidly turning a brownish-red. He had been killed by the other sparrows, by their hate for color and their instinct of belonging to a gray flock. Then, for the first time, I *understood*. . . ." (106)

In *The Painted Bird,* the story is given to Lekh, the bird trapper. Lekh, a strange loner himself, admires the freedom of the birds. His girl friend, Stupid Ludmila, a wild, untamed, half-simple woman who lives in the woods, is likened to a bird. When she disappears from time to time, in frustration Lekh paints trapped birds in gaudy colors and frees them among flocks of their own kind, where they are pecked to death by the drab brown flocks of their kin, just as Ludmila herself is finally killed by the drab village women, who resent her voluptuousness. The young boy who is protagonist of the novel is also, of course, a painted bird, with his hawklike nose and intense dark eyes, gaudy and outstanding among the bland, fair-complected peasants.

Kosinski has said in an interview, "In *No Third Path* you might have noticed the metaphor of the painted bird. That is when the embryo of my idea of the book was born.[6] The metaphor, which in *No Third Path* makes a nice point about the position of the individual in the collectivist society, becomes the central image in *The Painted Bird,* and indeed remains the central metaphor for all of Kosinski's writing, and for his life itself. It is a brilliant and timeless metaphor, and the expression "painted bird" may well stay in our vocabulary.

No Third Path

No Third Path is much more tightly constructed than *The Future Is Ours.*[7] Although in usual Kosinski fashion it consists of a number of superficially unrelated episodes, in fact it is strongly, almost essayistically theme-oriented. The book, masquerading as a bare sociological report, is a philosophical inquiry into human freedom. In particular, it debates whether freedom is to be found by the individual unrestrained by responsibility to or dependence upon anyone but himself, or by the member of a group who has given up his individuality completely to that group. Though the author employs the method of recording numerous interviews from people in different walks of life that he had in *The Future Is Ours,* here, in each interview, in each recounting of a person's lifestyle, this single issue is being examined from complementary perspectives. It scarcely needs to be said that this theme, of the individual versus the group, is central to most of Kosinski's fiction.

The theme is stated early. The secretary of the Komsomol cell in Moscow states with conviction:

"The average Soviet man . . . encounters in his everyday life much more creative emotion, excitement, and stimulation than the man who lives in any other system of society. Doubtless, the main reason for this difference is the role fulfilled in our lives by the collective and meetings." Every Soviet citizen attends "meetings" at least once a week, in which political issues are discussed, and individuals criticize themselves, or attack others in the group for deviating from collective goals. "They constitute, I'm sure, the paramount factor linking each of us to all others, the individual to society, and society to the individual. . . . No one of us may say that he thinks of himself in *his own* terms, because we evaluate ourselves by the eyes of *the others.* Those others are those who are closest to us, the participants in the same collectives, groups, and meetings, whom we meet face to face. In them, our fellow citizens, depends our happiness, our creative development, our tranquillity. . . . Wherever you go, you are in a collective! Wherever your collective goes, there you'll go also! Don't you perceive in this the shining essence of socialism?" (27)

An old and tested Party member "admits that the meeting is the fundamental element of Party work. 'Criticism and self-criticism,' he states with conviction, '—the decisive weapons of socialism—function at the meeting. The crucial problem of socialism, the relationship between the individual and society, and vice versa, finds its realization here. For after all what is the heart of the matter? It is that man should know *where* he is and *in what direction* he is moving. Who is to tell him that? Other people, of course. . . . Confronted by a critically disposed collective, the individual becomes a *socialized* individual, is enabled to assess himself from the standpoint of the interests of *other people,* of society, Party, ideology. . . . In this way the *criticism* of the individual by the collective leads to *self-criticism* by the individual" (32).

Gavrila, his political teacher, says,

"Remember . . . man is first of all a creature of comparison. In your country [Poland in 1956] everything is relative. Its socialist system has not yet hardened. That which Communists respect is repulsive to the Catholics and that which the Catholics respect, the Communists consider backward. The remnants of private trade are infecting everyone with a capitalist mentality, spreading opportunism and cynicism. As a result the society vegetates, all values are questioned. Here in the U.S.S.R. we have a uniform and universally respected hierarchy of values. A man knows which way is up and which way is down, where is the left and where is the right, what is good and what is bad. . . . Your Communist is still the hero of the future, but our Communist, the Soviet Communist, is the hero of the here and now, as well as the future. You're at the age when a choice must be made—this way or that. To drift is to degenerate." (69)

Kosinski tells us that Gavrila "was still convinced that man's internal life constitutes only a reflection of his environment—and not much more. And he was still unshaken in his conviction that the only true way for man to develop his versatile talents is in and through the collective" (70).

Over and over again we are shown how the collective dialectically purges the individual until he realizes, as Kosinski's professor at the university tells him, that "*true freedom is only necessity realized*" (103). Gavrila's advice for success: "*Follow the group.* . . . What could be simpler than that? In our society the price of being different is much too steep for anyone to afford it for long" (104).

It is at this point that Varvara tells the story of the painted bird (106–107).

Although Kosinski, as protagonist, has an ostensibly passive role as the mere recorder of these views, in fact the people are debating with him for his soul. He is being asked to stay in Russia and make his way with what Gavrila sees as the wave of the future. Implicitly, however, some others are presenting different views. The bookkeeper hiding in the toilets, for instance, is playing his dangerous game to maintain his difference, without paying too "steep" a price.

"All philosophy consists in this—" he continued, "to know how not to distinguish oneself. In the era of disturbances, changes, and struggles, one has to know how to sit still. This is very difficult," he emphasized, "very. . . . It is much more difficult than to be a revolutionary, which anyone can accomplish, right? I myself, for example, survived many times only because I was cautious. Till this very day I follow this principle: not to stand out, not to annoy anyone, to sit in the middle of the crowd and not at its edges. . . . Have you ever seen a large flock of sheep in motion? Which ones are the safest, which ones are not bitten by dogs, nor lacerate their flanks against the trees, nor are reached by the shepherd's whip? Those in the middle, in the very middle. . . . It is not so simple to stay there." (53)

But the cost is still steep. Not so steep perhaps as for the man who openly bucks the system and spends his life in forced labor camps, but steep enough. The bookkeeper continues: "'After all, what matters in life? What matters is to spend it peacefully, not to aggravate nerves— one's own or the other's. Life—' he searched for a definition, 'has to be waited through. . . . Get me?'" (53).

That is no life at all, of course, but a denial of life. But resigning oneself to "necessity" and joining the collective is even worse, a denial of personality.[8] Kosinski here begins to see that he must escape to one of the "bourgeois" societies where he will be left to himself. But left to himself for what purpose? When asked what his own goal in life is, he can only stumble. "I—I would like to depend on nobody. You know, to tailor my life to my own yardstick, and not to rifle around in ready-made-clothes stores . . ." (53).

This sort of fuzzy reply brings a stinging retort from Zina F., a girl he had once been close to:

"You are a little egoist, wrapped up in yourself! Your own nose, which you consider too long, your naturalistic remembrances of childhood and the war, your hatred of village life and primitive conditions, your 'exercise of intimacy'—all this causes the world of today to reach you in a *distorted image.* You refract it, as it were, in a prism. That most human and humanist institution which is the Soviet collective and our meetings, you consider as contrary to the nature of the 'free man!' But what is a free man if not just one of us, one of the people armed in Marxism-Leninism, people freer than anyone else, because they realize that liberty means the recognition of necessity? Can't you understand that at any of our meetings the most elevated motives come into play in man and are given external expression? That after any such meeting you become conscious of relaxation, of what in Greek poetry was termed *Katharsis,* purge! That you become conscious of the fullness of life, of the harmony reigning *between you yourself and your external life, life outside yourself, as it were.* What is your fullness of life, you poor, painted bourgeois? What is your *katharsis*—your success in life, your attitude toward the external world? Can you find such a fullness of life in the petit-bourgeois privacy of an apartment? Will it be given to you by intimate contact with a woman in whom you become transiently interested and with whom you can 'live it out?' Do you consider indifference toward world events, human progress, struggle for the victory of Communism in which men suffer more than you and I did during the last war, as your 'ambition in life?' Where will your 'philosophy of the distorted image' lead you in the long run? . . . To intellectual degradation and a spiritual void, to cultivating your wounded ego and the nightmares of your memories to the degree of causing pain to others and the 'right' of disregarding the others?" (58–59)

In fact, Kosinski himself, having opted for his "egotistical" freedom, his "petit-bourgeois privacy," having refused to recognize any "necessity" but his own, has very much devoted himself, in his novels, to trying to say what his goal is, to explain what his fullness of life and his freedom really do amount to. In the most direct way possible his entire literary career has been aimed at answering Zina F's passionately searching question.

Chapter Three
The Painted Bird and Notes of the Author

The Painted Bird is dedicated "To the memory of my wife, Mary Hayward Weir, without whom even the past would lose its meaning."

It was while he was living with her in such unimaginable wealth and splendor that the considerable amount of money he made from his books barely sufficed to pay for the tips during their travels, that he began writing *The Painted Bird*. "It was an attempt to somehow balance the reality of my past with the reality of my present. She, in turn, learned of my past through my writing."[1]

His words suggest an autobiographical impulse for writing the novel, but he has specifically denied such an impulse: "I did not have the intention of publishing my remorse or my personal memories . . . but solely of telling a story."[2]

It was in Lausanne, full of plaques commemorating international peace conferences which in the end had not been able to prevent the first and second world wars, that Kosinski renounced his social science studies for literature. "I knew . . . that contrary to politics, that offered only extravagant promises of a utopian future, fiction could represent existences such as they had been lived. . . . It was by pure chance that I had survived [the war years], and I was always conscious that hundreds of thousands of other children had been condemned."[3]

Actually, Kosinski tells me, *Steps* was intended to be his first novel. He set it aside, however, and began, in 1961, working on *The Painted Bird*. It grew to be a much larger novel than we have, but in revision he shortened it by a third, and continued changing it in galleys (the type was reset three times at Kosinski's expense). The book was finally finished in 1964 and published in the fall of 1965.

During his *Paris Review* interview, Kosinski was asked: "After the success of your early nonfiction, did you find it difficult to get your first novel, *The Painted Bird,* published?" Kosinski: "Yes, I did. When I had the manuscript in its finished form, the first step was to show the book to four friends of mine, who were all editors in very large, respectable publishing houses in New York. All four had an interest in my work because of the nonfiction, and all four told me in very plain language that in their view the novel was not publishable in America." Interviewer: "What were their reasons?" Kosinski: "That it was a book dealing with a reality which is alien to Americans, set in an environment that Americans cannot comprehend, and dealing with situations, particularly the cruelty to animals, that Americans cannot bear. No fiction could possibly alter all this, they said, and certainly not *The Painted Bird.* Their verdict was: Go back to writing nonfiction. I asked them who, in their view, would be the *least* likely publisher for this book. They said short of Vatican City, I should try Houghton Mifflin in Boston. I sent the manuscript, and a few weeks later they cabled that they wanted to publish it."[4]

The Painted Bird

The novel begins in Eastern Europe in 1939. It is the start of the Second World War and the Germans have invaded. The six-year-old protagonist (who is never named in the novel, just as the country in which the action takes place is never named) has been sent into the countryside by his parents to escape, they hope, the worst brunt of the war. But in the confusion he is cast adrift by himself, to live as he can, from the age of six until twelve, when the war finally ends. His problems are increased by the fact that he is dark haired and dark eyed and speaks the educated dialect, whereas the people he is living among are blond and blue eyed and speak a barely comprehensible peasant dialect. Because he is dark and different, he is "considered a Gypsy or Jewish stray" (2);[5] and since the Germans are rounding up Gypsies and Jews for the death camps, it is very dangerous for the peasants to harbor him. Therefore he is always treated with suspicion, and often with cruelty and violence.

He stays first with crippled, superstitious old Marta, who tells him his black eyes are evil and forbids him to look directly into her eyes or the eyes of any of her livestock. When she dies, he runs off into the forest, since she had told him any of the villagers would drown him like a kitten. But next day, hungry and exhausted (he is only six), he returns. He is beaten and tormented by laughing villagers till Olga the Wise buys him. She also tells him he is possessed by evil spirits, and he begins to believe it. After a while the villagers catch him, put him on a large catfish bladder, and set him adrift down the river. He lives wild in the forest, or is briefly and usually disastrously adopted by various peasants. At one point he stays with a carpenter who is fearful his black hair will attract lightning. When lightning indeed strikes the barn, the carpenter prepares to kill the little boy. Instead the boy manages to lead him to a bunker he knows of that is teeming with rats, and pushes the carpenter into it, where he is eaten alive.

The boy lives out the winter in the wild, wrapped in rags, stealing potatoes, and delighting in his freedom. When some boys come to beat him to death, he blows them up with a salvaged mine, and runs for it. Once or twice he is captured by the Nazis, but each time escapes.

As a penalty for causing an accident in the church, the peasants nearly drown him in a deep manure pit. He escapes, but he has become mute. He begins to feel the rule of the world is to do as much harm to others as possible. Briefly he lives with a voluptuous woman, Ewka. Though he is too young to be capable of actual sexual intercourse, he does everything she instructs him to do to delight her. He feels this is real love, but when he then witnesses her having sex with her brother, and even a goat, before the eyes of her father, he is disenchanted, and once more sets out on his own.

He continues to have adventures, always full of violence. The Germans are beginning to lose the war to the Russians. He sees a group of Kalmuks, Tartars in German uniforms, come up and have an orgy of raping and torturing villagers, and suddenly the Russians come, capture the Kalmuks, and crucify them.

The boy now travels with the Russian army as a sort of mascot. He worships them, especially the sniper Mitka, a solitary revenger like he is, and Gavrila, who gives him instruction in collectivist society.

He is put in an orphanage in a large city, where at long last he is discovered by his parents. He is still mute, and for a long time he is unable to live a normal child's life. He sleeps during the day and wanders the streets at night like a feral creature.

For therapy, his parents take him to the mountains, where he learns skiing. He is in the hospital after a serious skiing accident, no one is in the room, and the phone begins ringing. Suddenly he has an overpowering urge to speak. He answers the phone, and his voice has returned. For all his separateness, his cynicism and disillusion, his instinct to rejoin humanity, it seems, has won out.

How Autobiographical is *The Painted Bird?*

When Kosinski set out to write his story, he had the choice of writing a memoir, or a novel. As he has said repeatedly, he chose to write a novel, which is to say, a work of the imagination. It is as a novel that *The Painted Bird* will be discussed in the present book. Kosinski has also insisted, however, that the entire story is based on fact and was a way for his wife to learn of his past. Though the question of the nature of the work is not strictly a literary one (by which I mean that the novel is neither better nor worse for being, or not being, autobiographical), it is nonetheless a question of some interest, and I would like to address it briefly here. Of course, I cannot go very far, since we are dependent for what we know of Kosinski's early life on Kosinski's own statements, statements perhaps made faulty by memory, or confounded in his memory with his writing of similar incidents in *The Painted Bird*. Further, even if he was *trying* to write autobiography (which he was not), he has warned us that "what we remember lacks the hard edge of fact. To help us along we create little fictions, highly subtle and individual scenarios which clarify and shape our experience. The remembered event becomes a fiction."[6]

But with these warnings in mind, let us examine what he has said about his early life to see how it compares with the early life of the protagonist of his novel.

Kosinski was born in 1933, so that "the war was when I was from six to twelve."[7] In *Current Biography Yearbook,* we read that "When World War II broke out the Kosinskis sent their son eastward into the countryside for refuge."[8]

Two months after the German invasion of Poland in 1939 he was separated from his parents who assumed him dead. The next six years the young boy wandered throughout the villages in Eastern Poland believing he was either a Gypsy or a Jew, knowing the German penalties for harboring either. In 1942, at the age of 9, he lost his speech. In 1945, he was found by his parents in an orphanage, a half-mad, terrified, speechless child suddenly reunited with his family and civilization. For the next two years he remained speechless and slept in his clothes, refusing to leave the house during the day while at night he prowled the streets as he had done in Eastern Poland. Slowly, he began to recover and reenter civilization. By the time he was 14 he had become an avid skier, but he still could not talk. And, at 14, he had a serious skiing accident which hospitalized him for months. While he was recuperating he regained his speech.[9]

 The boy in the novel is six when, in the first weeks of the war, he is sent to the country by his parents for refuge. He is, like Kosinski, dark haired and dark eyed. He wanders from village to village. About midway on his journey, he loses his speech. Toward the end of the war he is rescued by the Russian army and kept for awhile under the care of an officer named Gavrila.[10] At the end of the war he is found by his parents. He is restless, sleeping by day and roaming the streets at night. For therapy, he is taken to the mountains, where he learns skiing. At an unspecified age after twelve, he has a skiing accident and, while recovering in the hospital, regains his speech.[11]

 The outlines are the same, but what of the details? "While denying that *The Painted Bird* is autobiographical," we are told, "Kosinski has admitted that 'every incident is true.'"[12]

 This is ambiguous. Does he mean every incident happened to him, or does he mean he witnessed every incident happening to someone, or does he mean he heard of these incidents happening to others, or does he simply mean the incidents have the sort of universal truth that characterizes all good literature?

 He has said that he set his novel "in the war-ravaged, small pocket of rural Europe, which I remember so intimately,"[13] and we find occasional confirmations by Kosinski that certain events in the novel were autobiographical. For instance, at one point some boys try to drown the narrator of the novel under the ice in a river. Kosinski has reported that "once, as a child, I was pushed under ice and barely survived."[14]

 The story of the "painted bird" itself—the story of someone painting a bird in bright colors, then liberating it, to see it pecked to death by its dull-colored fellows—Kosinski attributes to a girl in his nonfictional work *No Third Path* (see above, Chapter 2). That would suggest, then, that the incident of the young boy living with the bird catcher Lekh did not actually happen to Kosinski himself, or at least not exactly as he has written it in the novel.

And what of the horrendous revenges the protagonist of the novel perpetrates? Did six-year-old Kosinski actually push a peasant into a bunker teeming with rats so that he would be eaten alive? Did twelve-year-old Kosinski actually derail a train, killing and maiming scores of people, because a peasant had insulted him?

Kosinski is quiet on these questions.[15]

Perhaps a good many of the incidents in the novel—even the most traumatic[16]—actually happened to Kosinski himself. But others, like the bird catcher painting the trapped birds, may derive from overheard sources, and the more horrible of the protagonist's revenges have a quality of wish-fulfillment about them.[17] Once Gail Sheehy asked him: "In the last few years can you evoke a time, a moment, when you felt most intensely alive?" Kosinski: "I have such moments during most days of my life. I think the advantage of the imaginative life is that when reality slackens, at any time you can summon up some of these strong images—memories, fantasies, stories by other writers—that can speed it up. . . . In the moment of recalling these moments [of trauma] I was petrified again. . . . I guess that's what I meant by summoning dramatic images, a fusion of memory, fantasy, and emotion, without which that might have been a dull hour."[18]

Here, I suspect, is the truth of his novel: "A fusion of memory, fantasy, and emotion." We will never know the precise mixture of each. By now perhaps Kosinski himself does not know. The point is that *The Painted Bird* is a work of fiction, a work of art, and we take away from Kosinski's imaginative power when we think of his novel as simply autobiography. When Kosinski was asked what the difference was between an incident in one of his nonfiction books and the same incident in one of his novels, he said,

The difference is that my nonfiction grounds it [the incident] in a specific place—the U.S.S.R.—and by doing so torpedoes its immediacy, its proximity to the reader. On the other hand, the fiction invokes the reader directly. He cannot discard it by saying, "It already happened to someone else, hence it won't happen to me. I'm excluded; I'm a bystander." Perhaps the "nonfiction as literature" aims at nonevoking; it aims at reassuring the reader that the event had taken place or that it's a large historical process, hence that there's no direct threat to the reader. Fiction assaults the reader directly as if saying: It is about you. You are actually creating this situation when you are reading about it; in a way you are staging it as an event of your own life.[19]

In the discussion to follow I will show, I hope, that the novel is too finely crafted, too economically structured, to be a record of actual and untidy life. It is better, more philosophical, more universal, than any one life could actually be, just as Aristotle has told us that poetry is always superior to history.

But there is no denying that the fact that Kosinski may indeed have personally experienced the horrors of the novel gives the art of his novel a power and authority even beyond what it already had.

The Painted Bird as Picaresque Novel

The picaresque is a perennial literary form. It has some similarities to an epic like *The Odyssey,* and some similarities to a Greek romance like *The Golden Ass* of Apuleius. These two works both feature a central character who travels widely, meets various people, is confronted constantly with treachery or violence, and escapes (narrowly, and often painfully) by using his wits and his tremendous vitality, his unquenchable hunger for life at any cost. Sex is often as much of an ingredient as violence, and rapid and dramatic change seems to be the only principle that governs all the varied and episodic actions. Change, from the heights to the depths, and from the depths to deeper depths, and from deepest depths back to heights—and all ruled by the most quixotic chance.

The picaresque as a form, however, differs from the Greek romance and the epic by having a pícaro, an uneducated street urchin, for protagonist. *Lazarillo de Tormes,* a sixteenth-century Spanish work, is the prototypical picaresque novel. Lazarillo, an orphaned street urchin, is taken under the protection of a blind beggar who beats and starves him, but also teaches him the wiles that will help him to survive on the streets. Lazarillo lives by lying, cheating, stealing, and absorbing terrific beatings and other torments. His day is centered around getting enough food to keep from starving. He loses teeth and breaks ribs, but at the end of each day he has once more survived; and what is extraordinary is his energy, his willingness to take all life can deal out, and still look forward to the next day. There is a miraculous kind of freedom and even happiness in his life.

Lazarillo more or less directly gave rise to a picaresque tradition. Picaresque novels were written in Spain by such writers as Alemán, Quevedo, and Cervantes himself (even *Don Quixote* is a variety of picaresque). The vogue spread to Germany with works by Grimmelshausen, to France with works by Lesage, to England with works by Smollett, and to the present century with works by Gide, Céline, Mann, Bellow, and others. All these works are in a recognizable tradition, which is to say the authors of the later works had read and learned from earlier authors in the tradition, back to the Spanish sources. But the form is also a "natural" form, which is to say it has sprung up spontaneously from time to time, as the original form did, or as the novels of Defoe did, simply out of the fact that it reflects a particular and recurring social situation, and represents a certain recurring attitude toward life.

I think it would be accurate to describe *The Painted Bird* as a picaresque novel. All the hallmarks are there: the orphan stray using his wits and zest for existence to thread his way through a universe of lying, cheating, violence, perversion, in a world of seeming malevolence, but actually only of the most absolute chance.

The question arises: is Kosinski writing in the "tradition" of the picaresque? In other words, is he a trained and sophisticated writer self-consciously using this venerable form, or did he, as the very first writers of picaresque, come naturally upon the form because the form corresponded so exactly to the world as seen from his particular perspective?

Kosinski is a very sophisticated and self-conscious artist, conversant with the ancient and modern literatures of several languages and cultures. His writing and his conversation are filled with aesthetic theorizing, with detailed references to countless works of literature. And yet I suspect he came upon his picaresque structure himself, and not through study of a literary tradition. I have already suggested in Chapter 2 how the free-floating "outsider" protagonist, the episodic structure, and swiftly changing backdrop grew naturally out of the two nonfiction books. It seems to me just as obvious that the pícaro's philosophy of life has come to Kosinski just as naturally out of the tremendous ups and downs of his own life, writing the story of his mute and orphaned past while he lived in the incredible opulence of his life with Mary Hayward Weir.

The history of the last five hundred years in Western Europe is one of the feudal aristocracy's slowly being superseded economically and politically by the rising middle class. The movement, of course, was fiercely resisted by the waning aristocracy, as it saw its privileges gradually being lost. As Richard Byornson, in his study *The Picaresque Hero in European Fiction,* explains it, in the fourteenth and fifteenth centuries in Spain, the talented, ambitious, slowly rising middle class consisted mainly of people of Jewish origins who had converted to Christianity (those who had not converted had been expelled from Spain in the late fifteenth century). These *conversos* were at first accepted, but as they gained in wealth they gained in resentment from the poorer classes beneath them, and from the jealous aristocracy above them, and increasingly their rights were taken away from them, especially after the Inquisition began its search into the *limpieza de sangre* or "purity-of-blood" of the people. No matter how many generations a family had been good Christians, if an ancestor was suspected to have been Jewish, then the individual's position in society was made almost impossible.

With other avenues of expression closed off to them, some of the *conversos* turned to literature. The anonymous author of the prototype picaresque, *Lazarillo de Tormes,* may have been a *converso.* The author of *Guzman de Alfarache* (1559–1604), the first fully developed picaresque, Mateo Alemán, was certainly a *converso.* His novel is, under the surface, a plea for the freedom of the individual to find his own place in the rigid hierarchical society. It is written out of the experience, and from the point of view, of the talented but disenfranchised individual.[20]

Kosinski, the "inner emigré," the dark-complected Jew in the blond, Gentile society, a survivor of recent history's greatest experiment in "purifying the blood," shares with Alemán that overriding theme of the individual's need for freedom in a society that not only restricts him in movement, but will not even tolerate him in the few places it has left for him. The accident of his early life, and the nearly inevitable structure of his first two books, gave him the form of the picaresque, while his social position, like Alemán's, perhaps, gave him the picaresque point of view.

The Theme of Freedom: "The Painted Bird"

In one form or other, the motif or symbol of the "painted bird" is frequently present in Kosinski's writing. It is one pole of the debate between individual man and collective man, between freedom and safety, between expression and silence, between perilous and chance-filled life and anonymous living death.

We see it first in the prologue to the novel (italicized in the original): "The villages in which he was to spend the next four years differed ethnically from the region of his birth. The local peasants, isolated and inbred, were fair-skinned with blond hair and blue or gray eyes. The boy was olive-skinned, dark-haired, and black-eyed. He spoke a language of the educated class, a language barely intelligible to the peasants" (1). "He was considered a Gypsy or Jewish stray, and harboring Gypsies or Jews, whose place was in ghettos and extermination camps, exposed individuals and communities to the harshest penalties at the hands of the Germans" (2).

The boy is immediately, visibly different, arousing suspicion and fear. The lesson of being the odd man out, of the danger of being noticeable, is brought home to him over and over again. "Once a lonely pigeon joined the flock [of chickens]. He was clearly unwelcome. When he made a landing in a flurry of wings and sat amidst the chickens, they scurried away, frightened. . . . One day, when the pigeon was trying as usual to consort with the hens and chicks, a small black shape broke away from the clouds. The hens ran screaming toward the barn and the chicken coop. . . . Only the pigeon had no place to hide. . . . The hawk flew off smoothly, carrying in its beak the limp body of the pigeon" (4).

Later, when he lives with Lekh, the bird catcher, he sees the actual painted birds. "He would choose the strongest bird. . . . Lekh would turn the bird over and paint its wings, head, and breast in rainbow hues until it became more dappled and vivid than a bouquet of wildflow-ers. . . . When a sufficient number of birds gathered above our heads, Lekh would give me a sign to release the prisoner. It would soar, happy and free, a spot of rainbow against the backdrop of clouds, and then plunge into the waiting brown flock. . . . Dazzled by its brilliant colors, they flew around it unconvinced. . . . We saw soon afterwards how one many-hued shape lost its place in the sky and dropped to the ground." (44).

All elements of the motif are visible here: the bird is the strongest, the most beautiful. In its flight it is "happy and free." The "brown flock" is fearful and suspicious, and finally cruel. We see something of its psychology, perhaps, in Lekh himself, who only paints the birds when his girl friend, Stupid Ludmila, has disappeared into the forest for days, giving him no chance to see her. "Lekh would become possessed by a silent rage" (43). It is rage born of frustration that makes him cruel.[21] Ludmila is another version of the painted bird. She was an individualist from the start. When her father arranged a marriage between her and a man famous for his ugliness and cruelty, she refused. For a revenge, the jilted suitor trapped the young girl in a field and had her gang-raped by a number of peasants. Her brain addled, she lived like a wild thing in the woods, strong, full-blown and voluptuous, sleeping with any man or boy she chose. In her mad sensual freedom she was the antithesis of the drab, repressed village women, who hated her because once she had had their men, the men would never return. Lekh himself, though he loves her, is jealous of her freedom and paints the birds as a sort of revenge by indirection when she stays away too long. Eventually the village women trap Ludmila and savagely kick her to death (41–49).

Diametrically opposite to the painted bird, of course, was the bookkeeper Kosinski described in *No Third Path* (see above, Chapter 2). "All philosophy consists in this. . . to know how not to distinguish oneself. . . . I follow this principle: not to stand out, not to annoy anyone, to sit in the middle of the crowd and not at its edges." "By then he was in the bus and through a window I saw how deftly and energetically he elbowed his way through the closely packed passengers. When the bus moved, he was already in the 'very middle of the flock.'" It was in the "middle of the flock," in the middle of the great city of Moscow, hiding in the stalls of the men's rooms in great public buildings, that he claimed "while here I'm free as a bird." An odd kind of freedom, the freedom of a bird in a great communal cage. " 'Life—'he searched for a definition, 'has to be *waited through*. . . . Get me?' "[22]

The young narrator of *The Painted Bird* instinctively made the other choice. No matter what the risks of beating and deprivation and death, his real freedom and the full expression of himself were what mattered to him. Kosinski tells us that "by the age of eight, in terms of character and what I wanted to do, I was already completely formed."[23]

Ultimately, of course, and if Kosinski has an overriding theme through all his writing and all his life, this is it—the denial of life does not spare us from paying the debt, death. Collective safety is a sham: we die at any rate, and all we have avoided is not pain and death, but the possibility of freedom and life.[24]

The Theme of Freedom: The Comet

In addition to his wiles, his painfully gained experience, his determination, there was one tool absolutely necessary to the young narrator of the novel for his survival: his "comet." It

consisted merely of a one-quart preserve can, open at one end and with a lot of small nail holes punched in the sides. A three-foot loop of wire was hooked to the top of the can by way of a handle, so that one could swing it either like a lasso or like a censer in church. Such a small portable stove could serve as a constant source of heat and as a miniature kitchen. One filled it with any kind of fuel available. . . . By swinging the can energetically, one pumped air through the holes, as the blacksmith does with his bellows. . . . The comet was also indispensable protection against dogs and people. Even the most vicious dogs stopped short when they saw a wildly swinging object showering sparks. . . . Not even the boldest man wanted to risk his sight or having his face burned. . . . That is why the extinction of a comet was an extremely serious thing. . . . Matches were very scarce. (24–25)

Kosinski is a well-known, wealthy, successful novelist. Yet at any moment, however relaxed the situation, however surrounded he is by friends, in the trunk of his car, among canned goods, a drop-legged bed, and other emergency supplies, is "an odd-looking, charred, one-quart can with holes punched in its sides and a wire loop for a handle. This, the owner will explain, is an item essential to survival without human help."[25]

Kosinski also, we are told, carries "weapons" in the trunk of his car, but these he refers to as "'relative protection systems,' the 'strength of character' being the only absolute one."[26] The comet, then, is something other than a weapon. It is an actual, practical tool, of course, but it is more, it is a manifestation of the inner spark. It is the outward glow of the boy's determination to survive. But it is still more, it is his apartness itself, his individuality, that which is essential to survival "without human help." It is his essential aloneness, which is his independence and freedom. Without it he merges with the dark, merges with the animals; without it, when the dogs attack he can only hiss "like a snake" (27); without it he is at the mercy of the collective mass of man. And the more he merges with the dark, with the animals, with the collective mass, the less alive he is, the less chance he has, the more he despairs. But with the comet to fend off the dark, the animals, the other humans, he "felt perfectly safe" (26).

"At night, men and boys coming home would swing them with all their strength and let them fly into the sky, burning fiercely, like soaring red disks. The comets flew in a wide arc, and their fiery tails traced their courses. That is how they got their name" (26).

The Theme of Freedom: Being Alive

Severe winter set in. . . . No one wanted to keep me. Food was scarce and every mouth was a burden to feed. Besides, there was no work for me to do. . . . Wrapped in old rags, scraps of rabbit fur and horsehides, I wandered from one village to another, warmed only by the heat of the comet. . . . I carried on my back a sack of fuel, which I anxiously replenished at every opportunity. . . . When the sack was full I continued on my way with a feeling of contentment and security, twirling my comet and delighting in its warmth. Food was not difficult to find. The endless snow kept people in their huts. I could safely dig my way into the snowbound barns to find the best potatoes and beet-roots, which I later baked in my comet. . . . I slept in the forest, burrowing into a hollow beneath tree roots. . . . I loaded the comet . . . the fire lasted through the night and I could sleep in peace. (67–68)

When he is most alone, most independent, most directly engaged in the pure act of survival, he is also—no matter how hostile the environment—most free and happy, most alive.

"Finally, after a few weeks of milder winds the snow began to thaw and the peasants began to go outside. I had no choice . . . [but] to look for some remote village" (68).

With people out of their houses once more, he could no longer wander in freedom, stealing food with impunity. He would have to throw himself under the unreliable protection of some peasant, he would have to kiss feet and be humble and inconspicuous. He would, like the Bookkeeper, have to try to stay quietly in the middle of the flock, and "wait through" valuable months of his life. He would be forced into a position of life denial, and even then he would be in constant danger from the others, who would still notice his difference, the "painted bird" in their midst.

It was not the danger he feared—for danger could bring him closer to the intense experience of life—but the annihilation of self which was his only defense when he was forced to live with others on their terms.

Later, at the end of the war, in the relative safety of the orphanage, life suddenly began to lose its savor for him because there was not sufficient danger, and he had to manufacture thrills to return him to the happiness he had felt wandering alone and self-reliant in the deep snows:

As the train was approaching, I could hear and feel the thudding roar of the wheels through the rails and ties until I was shaking with them. When the locomotive was almost on top of me I flattened even more, and tried not to think. The hot breath of the furnace swept over me and the great engine rolled furiously over my back. Then the carriages rattled rhythmically in a long line, as I waited for the last one to pass. . . . It so happened that once, at the very moment of passing over a boy's body, the engineer had released some burning cinders. When the train was gone we found the boy dead, his back and head burned like an overbaked potato. . . . I recalled another occasion when the couplings hanging free at the end of the last carriage were longer than usual and they smashed the head of a boy. . . . Despite these grim recollections, there was something immensely attractive about lying between the rails with the train running above. . . . I felt within me life in a form as pure as milk. . . . Nothing mattered except the simple fact of being alive. (198)

The Theme of Freedom:
The Individual vs. the Collective

The Russian army sweeps through, mopping up the last of the German resistance. "I was somehow disappointed; the war seemed to be over" (163).

He had learned how to survive in the chaos of war, and ironically the end of the war meant starting over again to learn how to survive under changed conditions.

He was adopted by a Red Army regiment, and cared for mainly by two soldiers: Gavrila, "a political officer of the regiment," and Mitka, "known as 'Mitka the Cuckoo,' a sharpshooting instructor and a crack sniper" (167).

The two are good, honorable, generous men, almost the first two human beings in the boy's memory to treat him with decency and love. He returns their love, and accords them fierce loyalty and respect. He drinks in everything they say and do, and has no other goal than to be as much like them as possible.

But this is not possible, since they are themselves directly opposite to one another. In their different ways, they fight for the soul of the boy, and it is clear that he must choose between them.

Gavrila, the political officer, in simple, parablelike language, taught him the collectivist philosophy: "In the Soviet world a man was rated according to others' opinion of him, not according to his own. Only the group, which they called 'the collective,' was qualified to determine a man's worth and importance. The group decided what could make him more useful and what could reduce his usefulness to others. He himself became the composite of everything others said about him" (173). "How can an individual, Gavrila asked, presume to put his judgment ahead of that of the many?" (176). The boy responds: "I tried to memorize Gavrila's teaching, not to lose a single word. He used to maintain that to be happy and useful one should join the march of the working people, keeping in step with the others in the place assigned in the column. Pushing too close to the head of the column was as bad as lagging behind. It could mean loss of contact with the masses, and would lead to decadence and degeneracy. Every stumble could slow down the whole column, and those who fell risked being trampled on by the others . . ." (176).

But the philosophy is perilously close to that of the Bookkeeper's staying inside the flock. And the boy has had all too many experiences with putting himself into the hands of the others. "I felt lost in a maze. In the world into which Gavrila was initiating me, human aspirations were entangled with each other like the roots and branches of great trees in a thick forest . . . I was worried. What would happen to me when I grew up? How would I look when seen through the many eyes of the Party? . . . What would happen if the others, the collective, decided that I was better suited for some other work, such as deep-water diving, for example? Would it matter that I was now terrified of water because every plunge reminded me of my near-drowning under the ice? The group might think that it had been a valuable experience, qualifying me to train for diving" (175).

Mitka, his other teacher, is nicknamed "the Cuckoo," suggesting once more the "painted bird" theme. His profession of sniper behind enemy lines has caused him, like the boy, to perfect his natural traits of silence and aloneness, to rely on himself alone in a hostile countryside. The boy overhears one of Mitka's friends say, "Human being—that's a proud title. Man carries in himself his own private war, which he has to wage, win or lose, himself—his own justice which is his alone to administer" (186–87). The contrast with Gavrila's teaching is obvious. The boy learns, from Mitka's example, that "a man, no matter how popular and admired, lives mainly with himself. If he is not at peace with himself, if he is harassed by something he did not do but should have done to preserve his own image of himself, he is like the 'unhappy Demon.' . . . There were many paths and many ascents leading to the moral summit. But one could also reach the summit alone, with the help at most of a single friend, the way Mitka and I had climbed the tree. This was a different summit, apart from the march of the working masses" (187).

Crippled now by a German bullet, Mitka no longer went out on dangerous missions, but remained behind as the sharp-shooting teacher. But "at night I sometimes saw his wide-open, bright, piercing eyes staring at the triangular roof of the tent. He was probably reliving those days and nights. . . . Special German squads with trained dogs had searched for his hiding places, and the manhunts had covered wide circles. How many times he must have thought he would never return!

Yet I knew that these must have been the happiest days of Mitka's life" (180).

It is obvious which of these two won the boy's final allegiance.

The Theme of Revenge

The theme of revenge, violent, ugly, inordinate, is constant throughout Kosinski's writing. The theme seems to be dealt with quite programmatically in *The Painted Bird*. Let us see if we can follow it through all its ramifications.

At first, the impressionable boy witnesses others' acts of horrible revenge. He lives for a time with the Jealous Miller, a savage and taciturn man who regularly whips his wife out of suspicion that she is seeing other men. When he sees that a young plowboy appears to be attracted to his wife, he seizes his opportunity and suddenly scoops out both of the boy's eyes with a sharpened spoon. "The eye sprang out of his face like a yolk from a broken egg. . . . The eyeballs lay on the floor. I walked around them, catching their steady stare" (33). "The miller . . . squashed the eyeballs with his heavy boots. Something popped under his thick sole. A marvelous mirror, which could reflect the whole world, was broken. There remained on the floor only a crushed bit of jelly. I felt a terrible sense of loss" (34).

The horrified boy runs off, trying to memorize everything he sees, in case his eyes are one day plucked out. He sees revenge again when his next master, Lekh the bird trapper, angry when his wild-bird girl friend, Stupid Ludmila, is gone, paints the drab birds so that their fellows will peck them to death. But that is mild in comparison to what the village women do to her once they catch her, she who had robbed them of their men. "One of the women now approached, holding a corked bottle of brownish-black manure. . . . She kneeled between Ludmila's legs and rammed the entire bottle inside. . . . The other women looked on calmly. Suddenly with all her strength one of them kicked the bottom of the bottle sticking out of Stupid Ludmila's groin. There was the muffled noise of glass shattering inside" (48).

He next stays with a superstitious carpenter who believes that his black hair might attract lightning to the barn. When, during a storm, the barn actually is struck by lightning and burns, the carpenter prepares a sack to drown the boy in as if he were an unwanted kitten. This is the first time revenge has been turned directly onto the boy. But he tricks the carpenter to a bunker teeming with rats and manages to tip the carpenter into it, where he is eaten alive. The action, however, is less revenge on the boy's part than a desperate defensive effort (54–56).

His own first tentative act of aggression comes when some peasants turn him in to the German soldiers. He had always been told that his black eyes harbored evil spirits and had been forbidden to look at men or livestock. When a German officer looks at him dispassionately, "I looked straight into his eyes and wondered if this would cast an evil spell on him. I thought he might fall sick but, feeling sorry for him, I dropped my gaze" (62).

In the background a giant system of revenge was going forward, the death trains of the Nazis carrying the Jews to extermination camps. "The peasants . . . said the Lord's punishment had finally reached the Jews. They had deserved it long ago, ever since they crucified Christ. God never forgot. . . . Now the Lord was using the Germans as His instrument of justice" (84).

Later, a hideous revenge is visited upon the boy. He has become an acolyte in the church, but when it is his turn to carry the heavy Missal, he drops it. The outraged parishioners throw him into a dung pit, from which he barely escapes without suffocating, but finds the experience has left him dumb. He does not recover his voice for several years (122 ff).

At length the boy, thoroughly disenchanted with all men and their institutions, has a negative epiphany—evil people, he notices, have all the power and all the success, the Germans the most power and success of any:

I felt annoyed with myself for not having understood sooner the real rules of this world. The Evil Ones surely picked only those who had already displayed a sufficient supply of inner hatred and maliciousness. . . . I myself hated many people. How many times had I dreamed of the time when I would be strong enough to return, set their settlements on fire, poison their children and cattle, lure them into deadly swamps. In a sense I had already been recruited by the Powers of Evil. . . . I felt stronger and more confident. The time of passivity was over; the belief in good, the power of prayer, altars, priests, and God had deprived me of my speech. . . . Now I would join those who were helped by the Evil Ones. I had not yet made any real contribution to their work, but in time I could become as prominent as any of the leading Germans. (136–38)

The boy witnesses one more horrendous act of revenge. The Germans are losing the war. They are leaving; the Soviet army is shortly to arrive. Suddenly, at the last minute, "a band of mounted men rode up to the village. There were a hundred of them, perhaps more. They seemed to be one with their horses; they rode with marvelous ease, without any set order. They wore green German uniforms with bright buttons and forage caps pulled down over their eyes" (157). These are the dreaded Kalmuks, deserters from the Soviet army since the Soviets would not allow them to loot and rape in their time-honored manner. They had joined the Germans, and by the Germans "were sent to villages and towns that were to be punished for some noncompliance and, particularly, to those towns that lay in the path of the advancing Red Army" (157). For page after sickening page they murder the men and torture and rape the women and children, even the infants. The boy's ribs are cracked by a rifle butt, but he manages to escape and hide himself.

Ironically, when they first arrived, "as I looked at them, I felt great pride and satisfaction. After all, those proud horsemen were black-haired, black-eyed, and dark-skinned [like me]. They differed from the people of the village as night from day. The arrival of these dark Kalmuks drove the fair-haired village people almost insane with fear" (157–158). But their horrible acts quickly disenchant and disgust the boy, and he now deplores his darkness and feels he understands why everyone treats him so badly because of it.

He is much more satisfied when, revenge piled on revenge, the Soviet soldiers arrive, run the Kalmuks down, and crucify them, hanging them upsidedown from trees till they suffocate from the blood swelling into their heads (164–65).

The boy now travels with the Russian army, looked out for by Gavrila and Mitka. At one village near which they camp, some of the soldiers—close friends of Mitka, the sniper—get into a fight with villagers over their women. The villagers, greatly outnumbering them, attack them with axes, killing four and wounding others. The soldiers are forbidden to mix with the hostile villagers, and after a while it seems the incident has been forgotten. But one night Mitka, crippled a year earlier by a German bullet, gets the boy to help him while he struggles to a vantage point outside the village. They get up into a tree, and Mitka, with his long-range accuracy, shoots down several villagers, the boy loyally aiding him in this first professional lesson in revenge. During his life in the villages, the boy had been kept by one sadistic master who enjoyed making him hang from the ceiling by his hands while a savage dog leapt up trying to tear him apart. When the boy spots a similar-appearing dog in the village, he tries to get Mitka to shoot it also, but Mitka, not understanding his motive, refuses, and is quite indignant that the boy would think of shooting something outside the legitimate boundaries of revenge (187).

He understands Mitka's philosophy of revenge: "A man, no matter how popular and admired, lives mainly with himself. If he is not at peace with himself, if he is harassed by something he did not do but should have done to preserve his own image of himself, he is like the 'Unhappy Demon, spirit of exile, gliding high above the sinful world'" (187). In the period before the revenge Mitka had been sick and miserable. Now, "he was mild and cheerful as before" (188).

With all this example and instruction, nothing is left for the boy but to begin practicing his own manly art of revenge.

At first he does so in small ways. When he is placed in the orphanage, he is still proudly wearing the cut-down Red Army uniform given him. It is filthy and foul-smelling, but he refuses to take it off. When nurses finally overpower him and take it off, he goes to some Russian soldiers he finds in the streets and claims that the people who had taken his uniform were landlords and had beaten him because of his Soviet uniform. The soldiers go back and terrorize them, and after that he is left alone (191–92).

But these small revenges build up to the big one. He has befriended a boy at the orphanage known as The Silent One. The mute boy and The Silent One are almost like twins. One day they are at an outdoor market when the boy accidentally knocks over the contents of a stall. The owner savagely beats him, knocking out several of his teeth, and throws him on a garbage heap, injuring and humiliating him.

Mitka's teachings were always with him:

A man should never let himself be mistreated, for he would then lose his self-respect and life would become meaningless. What would preserve his self-respect and determine his worth was his ability to take revenge on those who wronged him.

A person should take revenge for every wrong or humiliation. . . . Only the conviction that one was as strong as the enemy and that one could pay him back double, enabled people to survive. . . . It was quite simple: if someone was rude to you and it hurt you like a whiplash, you should punish him as though he had lashed you with a whip. If someone slapped you and it felt like a thousand blows, take revenge for a thousand blows. The revenge should be proportionate to all the pain, bitterness, and humiliation felt as a result of an opponent's actions. (194)

The boys learn how to throw a switch on the tracks where the railroad brings the farmers to town to work their market stalls. The boys (it is mainly at The Silent One's instigation) throw the switch, derailing the train into the river. Dozens are killed or injured. When they get back to their dormitory: "I took a good look at The Silent One. There was no trace of tension in his face. He looked back at me, smiling softly. If it had not been for the bandage over my face and mouth I would have smiled too" (203).

But when they rush back to the market on the next market day and thread their way through the stalls—many of them closed and marked with crosses—they suddenly see the stall of their tormentor open; the man, unharmed, at work. They run off in anguish: "As soon as we reached the road, The Silent One fell down on the grass and cried as though in terrible pain, his words muffled by the ground. It was the first time that I had heard his voice" (203).

What are we to make of this story? The conventional moral would be that revenge is not worth it, that it only adds more evil to a world that already has a sufficiency. But this apparently is not the point. The boys' anguish is not at the unnecessary death and injury they have caused; it is only that they have missed their target. Revenge itself is not bad. Only, this particular attempt failed to achieve its purpose.

A little later, when the boy is reunited with his parents and beginning to live something like a normal life, the usher at a theater, not understanding he had already bought a ticket, rudely manhandles him and throws him out. He returns later, climbs to the top of an adjoining building, and drops a bottle to the sidewalk. When the usher comes over to investigate, he drops two bricks on him. Like Mitka, he believes that "a man should never let himself be mistreated, for he would then lose his self-respect and his life would become meaningless" (194).

The Theme of Education

Any novel which has as its protagonist a young boy who grows older during the course of it is almost willy-nilly an education novel (often called a *Bildungsroman*), for young boys are voracious of experience, and almost everything that happens to them happens for the first time, and teaches them something new about their world.

But education has a special importance in *The Painted Bird*. "It was by pure chance that I had survived, and I was always conscious that hundreds of thousands of other children had been condemned."[27] So Kosinski tells us about himself, but if we can take the experience of the boy in the novel as parallelling Kosinski's experience, we can say it was not "pure chance" that he survived. The boy in the novel, at any rate, was a survivor in a more positive sense, his own cunning and desire to survive being, in most cases, more important than "pure chance." In a situation of unremitting violence and deprivation, the desire to continue can be the most important element, and the strength to maintain psychic health can be a greater test than the strength to maintain bodily health.

I have suggested that *The Painted Bird* is a picaresque novel. The unnamed young protagonist is certainly a picaresque hero in the sense that he absolutely accepts the world he lives in. Although he experiences some very low ebbs, he never curses the world itself or finds it unfair or unjust to him. He accepts it on its own terms, and continually tries to learn its rules, its central principles, so that he can function effectively in it. The key to his psychic health is his acceptance: his assumption of the normality of his situation.[28]

Very early on, of course, he learns his first lesson—that he is different. His first masters, Marta the cripple and Olga the Wise, teach him that his dark hair and eyes, his olive skin, are the signs "that I was possessed by an evil spirit, which crouched in me like a mole in a deep burrow. . . . Such a person as I, possessed of this evil spirit, could be recognized by his bewitched black eyes. . . . I could stare at other people and unknowingly cast a spell over them" (16). It is a form of power to be different from others, but also it is perilous, as the several examples of "painted birds" demonstrate to him. Therefore he learns well "the two things which, according to Olga, were necessary for survival without human help. The first was a knowledge of plants and animals, familiarity with poisons and medicinal herbs. The other was possession of fire, or a 'comet' of one's own" (24).

It is after this, living on his own during the winter, that he learns that independence and freedom are not only necessary to a wild bird like him, but they are the sources of keenest happiness.

His strength and resolve are only twice shaken. The first time is when he is caught and placed in the hands of an SS officer. The officer's resplendent "soot-black uniform," the proud peak of his cap with its "death's-head and crossbones," make him almost synonymous with death, but a death so beautiful and controlled in comparison to the wretched disorganization of life that the boy is very attracted to it:

I could not tear my gaze from him. His entire person seemed to have something superhuman about it. Against the background of bland colors he projected an unfadable blackness. In a world of men with harrowed faces, with smashed eyes, bloody, bruised and disfigured limbs, among the fetid, broken human bodies, of which I had already seen so many, he seemed an example of neat perfection that could not be sullied. . . . I thought how good it would be to have such a gleaming and hairless skull instead of my Gypsy face. . . . I felt like a squashed caterpillar oozing in the dust, a creature that could not harm anyone yet aroused loathing and disgust. . . . I had nothing against his killing me. . . . I knew my fate was being decided . . . but it was a matter of indifference to me. (100–101)

Against the transience and chaos of life, he hungers for the perfection of death. He is more disappointed than relieved when a priest saves his life. "He looked even shabbier than before. His cassock was a miserable thing in comparison with the uniform adorned by the death's-head" (101).

At this low ebb of weakness, he can no longer stand by himself. The Church had brought him back to life, and so for a time he gives his entire allegiance to the Church. The priest unfortunately leaves him in the care of a sadistic farmer who beats him constantly for no reason and makes him support himself from ceiling hooks by his slowly weakening hands while the farmer's savage wolfhound leaps up and tries to attack him. Appropriately, the dog's name is Judas, for almost everything about his experience with the Church will be a betrayal of one sort or other.

He has very little understanding of the Mass or the role of the priest. "All of this to me was magic, more splendid and elegant than Olga's witchcraft" (106). But he does finally learn

that those who say more prayers earn more days of indulgence, and that this was also supposed to have an immediate influence on their lives. . . . Suddenly the ruling pattern of the world was revealed to me with beautiful clarity. I understood why some people were strong and others weak, some free and others enslaved, some rich and others poor, some well and others sick. The former had simply been the first to see the need for prayer, and for collecting the maximum number of days of indulgence. . . . I stopped blaming others; the fault was mine alone, I thought. I had been too stupid to find the governing principle of the world of people, animals, and events. But now there was order in the human world, and justice too. One had only to recite prayers. . . . (111–12)

But then, always an empiricist, always testing his theories against the facts of his world, he notices that the priest himself falls ill. "I was astonished. The priest must have accumulated an extraordinary number of days of indulgence during his pious life, and yet here he was lying sick like anybody else" (114).

It is then that, working as an acolyte, he drops the Missal, and the congregation turns on him in fury and tries to drown him in the dung pit, and he loses his speech, a sort of ultimate rejection of communion, of living collectively with others: "There must have been some cause for the loss of my speech. Some greater force, with which I had not yet managed to communicate, commanded my destiny. I began to doubt that it could be God. . . . God had not reason to inflict such terrible punishment on me. I had probably incurred the wrath of some other forces" (126).

If God, then, is not the main power of the universe, what is? For a short time, he thinks that love might be a great power. His new master, the farmer Makar, has a daughter, Ewka, who teaches the little boy ways to touch and kiss her body that send her off in writhing paroxysms of passion. He uses all his subtlety and delicacy and imagination to please her and feels he has a very special relationship with her. But when one day he sees her coupling just as eagerly, and in rapid succession, with a goat and with her brother, "something collapsed inside me. . . . All these events became suddenly clear and obvious. . . . They explained the expression I had often heard people use about people who were very successful in life: 'He is in league with the Devil'" (135). He goes on:

Only those with a sufficiently powerful passion for hatred, greed, revenge, or torture to obtain some objective seemed to make a good bargain with the Powers of Evil. . . . I felt stronger and more confident. The time of passivity was over; the belief in good, the power of prayer, altars, priests, and God had deprived me of my speech. My love for Ewka, my desire to do anything I could for her, also met with its proper reward. Now I would join those who were helped by the Evil Ones. (136–37)

Yet when he witnesses the Kalmuks, personifications of evil (as the SS Officer personified death), torturing, raping, murdering, the Kalmuks he had momentarily identified with because they were dark like him, "I crept deeper into the bushes, overwhelmed by dread and disgust. Now I understood everything. I realized why God would not listen to my prayers, why I was hung from hooks, why Garbos beat me, why I lost my speech. I was black. My hair and eyes were as black as these Kalmuks'. Evidently I belonged with them in another world. There could be no mercy for such as me" (160).

Here is his very lowest moment. He is not only at his lowest spiritual ebb, but at his worst physically. A Kalmuk had crushed his chest with a blow from his rifle butt. The Red Army arrives, rounds up the Kalmuks, and hangs them upsidedown from trees. He drags himself to the site: "A gust of wind shook the trees. The bodies swung shivering in widening circles. . . . I looked around for death, for I felt its breath in the air. . . . It was nearer to me than ever. I could almost touch its airy shroud, gaze into its misty eyes. It stopped in front of me. . . . I hoped it would take me along to the other side of the forest. . . . I reached out my hand, but death vanished among the trees" (165).

And he has come through. The war has ended. The novel pivots at this point; from this darkest episode it begins climbing slowly toward the light. But his education continues.

As I discussed above, Gavrila and Mitka fight for his allegiance, the first arguing for the collective life, the second for the life of solitary self-reliance, and for the ethic of revenge.

Mitka, of course, wins; but then the boy's parents reclaim him, and new claims are made upon his freedom. Not love and loyalty for the abstract collective, but those more subtle and binding demands made by blood—the love of family. These demands he finds suffocating and unbearable; so he wanders the streets at night, making friends with the desperate street people, among whom he feels freer and more alive. He is coming now to what he believes is his final philosophical stance, his ultimate picture of the world:

Every one of us stood alone, and the sooner a man realized that all Gavrilas, Mitkas, and Silent Ones were expendable, the better for him. It mattered little if one was mute; people did not understand one another anyway. . . . Everyone thought only of himself. His emotions, memory, and senses divided him from others as effectively as thick reeds screen the mainstream from the muddy bank. (212)

But another conclusion cuts right across this one. Injured in a skiing accident and recovering in a hospital bed, the mute boy hears the phone ring: "Somewhere at the other end of the wire there was someone, perhaps a man like myself, who wanted to talk with me. . . . I had an overpowering desire to speak. . . I opened my mouth and strained. Sounds crawled up in my throat. . ." (213).[29]

What is *The Painted Bird* About?

To a greater or lesser degree, the novel *The Painted Bird* follows actual events in Kosinski's life. At this distance in time perhaps Kosinski himself no longer knows to what extent the novel is autobiographical. He gets very annoyed, however, by people who are interested in his novel only as autobiography, and I think his annoyance is justified. I have been trying to suggest that under the novel's apparently loose, episodic surface it is actually quite tightly and programmatically structured. But toward what end? What theme is being generated? What, in other words, is the book about?

As I have already reported in Chapter 2, Kosinski has said he wanted "to use 'the stones' of his childhood 'to build a new wall,' to take 'the literal and turn it into something symbolic. . . . Just as the setting is metaphorical, so do the characters become archetypes.'"[30]

During his *Paris Review* interview, he commented in passing, "I think it is childhood that is often traumatic, not this or that war" (*PR*, 194). The interviewers let the statement go by, but I suspect it may be Kosinski's most profound statement about his novel. Perhaps, after all, the novel is best read as an allegory of childhood, and the war—as so often in works of fiction—as symbolic of the struggle and engagement with life. In modern societies—Dickens was among the first to point this out to us—children, who are small, weak, powerless, ignorant of adult ways, are deeply alienated from the ruling adult society. Learning to live in that society can be a deeply scarring struggle in enemy territory. Reconciliation and reopening of communications come, if at all, only with the slow, painful dawning of maturity.

Notes of the Author on *The Painted Bird*

Though published as a single volume by Kosinski's own Scientia-Factum, *Notes of the Author* can scarcely be considered as one of Kosinski's "books." It is in reality a brief (twenty-two pages) essay on his novel *The Painted Bird*. Kosinski has often stated that he does not like to discuss his works after they are written, feeling that the work itself is his full statement, and any other statements are for the readers and critics to make.[31] I asked him how it was, then, that he published this essay, which is essentially a critical analysis of his novel.

What happened, he explained to me, is that he wrote a series of letters to his German-language publisher (who happened to be a Swiss skiing friend) about, or on subjects touching on, *The Painted Bird*. The publisher, without Kosinski's knowledge or permission, casually added these letters as notes to the end of *The Painted Bird* when he published it. After that, Kosinski had no choice but to print the essay in English and put it on sale to at least thirteen people in order to protect his copyright on the material in the United States.

The notes, as they are gathered—and, remember, without Kosinski's permission—seem to have as a main objective the downplaying of *The Painted Bird* as autobiography, and a stressing instead of its literary structure and intention.

Kosinski's argument against reading the novel as simple autobiography is first of all that autobiography itself, since it is based on memory, is impossible to write without making it into fiction: "We fit experience into molds which simplify, shape and give them an acceptable emotional clarity. *The remembered event becomes a fiction, a structure made to accommodate certain feelings.* If there were not these structures, art would be too personal for the artist to create, much less for the audience to grasp. *There is no art which is reality; rather, art is the using of symbols by which an otherwise unstateable subjective reality is made manifest*" (11).

A second distancing, or fictionalizing of experience occurs, in the case of *The Painted Bird,* because an adult is writing about the experiences of a child, and an adult is able to see pattern, the total fabric of experience, where the child can only see the discrete, apparently random events as they are actually impinging on his consciousness one by one. "Events to the child are immediate: discoveries are one-dimensional. . . . But to the adult the vision of these memories is multi-dimensional. Hunger is no longer an intermittent memory as it was then, fear is no longer an irregular pulse as it once was. These are no longer absorbed by the body as the changing fortunes of the passing days. Rather they appear now to have been the seams and the bindings of a way of life. . . . The events have lost their isolation, have merged and fluxed, ebbed and flowed through the author's mind like tides. He gives the cloth of his experience, not merely threads" (15).

Kosinski does not, however, want to go too far in denying a factual base for his novel. "The content of the book presents problems. Expanded fact is not fiction; enriched memory is not simple invention" (14).[32]

Kosinski proceeds to an analysis of the novel, stressing the artifice in its structure. "In THE PAINTED BIRD one textual device frequently employed is the use of a natural subplot" (17). Much that happens to his human characters is repeated in the natural world. For instance, in one scene the sexual attraction between two characters is acted out at the same time by two cats coupling violently; the protagonist is parallelled with the painted bird, and so on.[33] Or, another literary device, traditional story motifs are often inverted in the novel, to stress the tragedy of the situation: The Silent One and the protagonist would normally occur in an idyll of childhood, not, as in this novel, in an orgy of revenge; there is a murder at a wedding, which then becomes a funeral; the parents' rediscovery of their long lost child brings no happiness.

In a long section of the essay, Kosinski attempts to defend the brutality of the peasants. Their brutality, he reminds us, has allowed them to endure against all odds, their distrust of strangers has been repeatedly reinforced by its demonstrated survival value. And finally, he points out, the cruelties of the "primitive" peasants are as nothing beside the mass extermination being carried out by the civilized city-educated Western Europeans with their millennia of culture behind them. Since the civilized Nazis would penalize these peasants with instant death for harboring a dark-complected Gypsy or Jewish child, "it seems, therefore, that all the adults in this book are positive heroes, because they did not kill the Boy" (25).

The Boy as Christ

In a brief aside, Kosinski makes a suggestion that, in my opinion, no other reader could have; a suggestion that possibly evidences one of Kosinski's intentions in the novel: "Perhaps, in their deepest thoughts lies the belief that while both the arrival and the appearance of the Boy endanger them, yet he *may* have been sent to save" (24). That faintest hint of the boy as a Redeemer may have been the reason, Kosinski suggests, that the congregation turned on the boy so murderously when the Missal slipped from his hands during the church service—his clumsiness evident proof that their expectations would be disappointed.

But if the young boy, dropped parentless and mysterious into their midst, began as a blameless vessel to absorb all their sins, by the end there has been a terrible irony—at least according to Kosinski's analysis of the novel. By the end he has taken on the sins of the others so fully that he has become evil himself. The bringer of Love has become the avatar of Hate. "Of all the characters he alone hates consciously, continously, and most deeply; he desires and thirsts to hate others for all that had happened to him in this world" (25).

"This hatred, this particular genre of revenge" (27), is his legacy, the inheritance the modern world has given its children. Kosinski suggests there is a sort of solitary strength in it. "To possess hate is to possess great power, and the wielder of that power has control of magnificent gifts" (27). Is it sardonic irony on Kosinski's part, the creation of a failed Christ made absolute by hatred? Or does he mean, simply, realistically, that in our world a certain ferocity is necessary if you would be a survivor? There is no doubt that revenge continues to play an important part in all of Kosinski's subsequent novels.

But at the same time, we cannot forget—what Kosinski in his analysis seems to have forgotten—the sudden cutting away of irony at the end of *The Painted Bird,* when the words are crawling up the boy's throat in his effort to communicate with another human being.[34]

This interpretation suggests that *The Painted Bird* does not end upon a heavy note of hatred. Let me quote portions of the final paragraph, and give Kosinski's interpretation of it, as he sent it to me, commenting on my interpretation: "I opened my mouth and strained. Sounds crawled up my throat . . . I began to recite to myself words and sentences, snatches of Mitka's songs. The voice lost in a faraway village church had found me again and filled the whole room. I spoke . . . enraptured by the sounds that were heavy with meaning . . . confirming to myself again and again and again that speech was now mine and that it did not intend to escape through the door which opened onto the balcony" (213). Kosinski suggests, "'The voice lost in a faraway village church' might now speak of 'manure pits.' 'Snatches of Mitka's song'? Mitka is *the avenger* of the novel! 'Balcony' is the place reserved for those who speak to the masses (leaders, political figures, mob crusaders, etc.). The Boy's speech 'did not intend to escape through the door which opened to the balcony.' Perhaps the communication will be 'to' others rather than 'with' them. . . ." The suggestion, I suppose, is that language, now that he has it back, will be an aid in his revenges, will help him express his hatred. Well, Kosinski himself uses his best form of communication, his novels, to alert, to warn, to save. Though his experiences were similar to the boy's, he has somehow, it would appear, emerged with a more positive attitude toward mankind. No: a page earlier, at the nadir of his cynicism, the boy had said that "it mattered little if one was mute: people did not understand each other anyway." A page later, when he suddenly sees the value of talking with or to another, "perhaps a man like myself," no matter with what load of hatred, it seems to me it still must be read as a step toward, not farther away from, human communion, and without that, I think the boy has not really been a survivor.

Chapter Four
Steps and The Art of the Self

Kosinski, speaking of himself in the third person, tells me that he "planned *Steps* to be his first novel, since it clearly states its purpose, its esthetics, but he decided he was too close to some of the events he wanted to portray in it (his Polish as well as his American past: ski instructorship as well as trucking in the USA) and so in 1961 he began work on *The Painted Bird*—'his more remote past.'"[1]

When *Steps* finally appeared in 1968, it won the National Book Award, and has gone on to sell over 4 million copies. There is a wonderful story connected with the book. Ten years later, in 1978, a free-lance writer named Chuck Ross, interested in what chances a new and unknown writer had of breaking into the market, for an experiment sent out a copy of the manuscript of *Steps,* under a different title, and under an assumed name, to fourteen different publishers and numbers of literary agents. None of the publishers (even Kosinski's own publisher who had originally published *Steps*) recognized the novel and none would even consider it for publication, and none of the literary agents thought it was worth his while to try to handle it.[2]

I suspect that if Kosinski had indeed written *Steps* first, and had not had behind him the highly successful and profitable *The Painted Bird*, he may have had as much trouble getting *Steps* accepted as Chuck Ross did. The book is very difficult—not in terms of its scenes, which have an almost hallucinatory clarity, but in terms of trying to put the scenes together into a coherent pattern. Kosinski himself feels that "it facilitates the act of reading *less*" than any other of his works. "It offers 'steps,' but refuses to tell whether it is a 'staircase'—and if it is one, where does it lead."

My object in this chapter wll be to try to make some sense of the structure of the novel.

Steps

The novel consists of thirty-five incidents, or vignettes, for the most part unconnected causally, though perhaps tonally similar. Interspersed with these, and the chief recurring element of the book, are thirteen italicized dialogues of a man and woman involved in intricate pre- and postcoital discussions of various extreme refinements of sensuality. Since there is seldom an ongoing "plot" in the usual sense, and since we cannot even be sure if the central character of each episode is the same person or not, the book is very difficult to summarize. But perhaps the flavor of the book can be given if I describe the first few episodes.

1. The narrator is a rich traveler. He stops in a poor village, where he tells an orphan girl that if she comes with him she will never need to work again. He buys her clothes, wine, takes her to a hotel. She moistens her lips and with her unsteady gaze seeks out his own.

2. The narrator is an archaeological assistant, stranded on an island with no money, and not knowing the language of the natives. He must prostitute himself to hideous fat women in return for food.

3. The narrator is a ski instructor near a sanatorium. He begins visiting a dying woman. She only lets him make love to her from a distance, their two images touching in the mirror. The nurse says people like him are hyenas, feeding on flesh. The woman is weaker after each of his visits.

4. The narrator goes to a show where peasants pay huge sums to see a frail young girl take on a large farm animal, not believing she can endure it. She starts screaming at the end, but he is not sure if this is real, or play-acting.

5. The narrator is impotent with an exciting lover, so he goes to a whore who caresses him just as he would himself; then he suddenly realizes the whore is a man.

6. While he's in the army the men play a game around a table, all with strings tied to their organs. One man pulls a string and they bet on how far it can be pulled without the soldier revealing who he is. Some men ruin themselves for life to win the prize. Then they find out two men are cheating, one tying the string to his leg. They take them out and crush their organs to a pulp with stones.

7. Soldiers talk about never knowing what a woman is thinking when they make love. He thinks of his girl friend, who was furious with him when he answered the phone and talked to a friend while continuing to make love. She thought his erection should be spontaneous rather than a controlled act of will that made everything predictable.

8. A man skips out on a parade, is suddenly caught naked, and salutes the flag, then notices he has an erection. He still manages to get off with only minor punishment.

At this point the first of the italicized dialogues occurs. The woman asks the man if circumcision doesn't make a man less sensitive, less responsive and thinks it is a cruel thing to do to a baby.

The novel goes on in this fashion to the end. Only the last vignette breaks the pattern, by being in the third person. "She" is in the hotel alone. She has been deserted by him, or so it appears. she goes out into the ocean and dives deeply, apparently suicidally. We do not know if "she" is the *she* of the italicized episodes, though we assume she is. We do not know if he is the *he* of the dialogues, the *I* of the episodes, or whether or not the *I*'s of the various episodes are the same person.[3]

The Structure of *Steps*

The novel seems quite innovative in its loose, almost structureless form, but actually in many respects it goes back to the first two nonfiction books (*The Future Is Ours, Comrade,* and *No Third Path*), discussed in Chapter 2, in that it consists of a series of episodes linked by a freely moving first-person narrator who in each episode finds himself in a different place, a different situation, interacting with different people. And of course, since *The Painted Bird* is also patterned after the earlier nonfiction books, the individual episodes in that book are similar to episodes in *Steps*. Indeed, some of the episodes in *Steps* might actually have been episodes originally written for the nonfiction books or *The Painted Bird* and later left out.

What is unique to *Steps* and makes it appear so different from the earlier books is that its episodes are self-reflexive. They look at themselves alone; and as the reader comes to realize that episode does not lead to episode, but that each stands alone, he begins himself to give each episode his full attention, rather than looking ahead to see what it will lead to. The separate vignettes in the nonfiction books, interesting in themselves, nonetheless took on larger interest by being part of an interrelated theme, the exposition of collective life, and the debate between whether man was freest in the controlled society, where his goals were clearly marked out for him, or in the totally free society, where he must discover his own goals. The vignettes in *The Painted Bird* all pushed forward to the telling of a story of the boy's learning to be a man and finally a human being, in spite of the world that tried so steadily to dehumanize him.

In *Steps,* the incident is there, *period,* and we look at the incident, *period.*

Nevertheless, and at the risk of falsifying Kosinski's intention, I believe I can facilitate my discussion of the novel if I try to schematize the arrangement of the episodes, and divide the episodes up by type. Chapters or sections are not numbered in the book. Simply, episodes are separated from each other by an asterisk, and occasionally there is a page break, suggesting that a new section of incidents has begun. There are five such section breaks, which I have numbered I, II, III, IV, V, each with a varying number of incidents. Thirteen of the incidents are the recurring italicized dialogues. Therefore I have numbered the incidents in my copy of *Steps* as follows:

I: 1, 2, 3, 4, 5, 6, 7, 8, 9, 10, *11,* 12, 13, 14, *15, 16,* 17, *18,* 19, *20,*
II: *1,* 2, 3, 4, 5, 6
III: *1,* 2, 3, 4, 5, 6, 7, 8
IV: 1, 2, 3, 4, 5, *6, 7, 8,* 9
V: *1,* 2, 3, *4,* 5

Almost all the incidents fall into one of three obvious patterns, or motifs, with sometimes more than one motif to an incident.

First of all, seventeen of the incidents[4] can be considered to be in some respects "autobiographical." That is, they include scenes of a young boy orphaned in Eastern Europe, being badly treated by peasants, very like scenes in *The Painted Bird* and presumably like Kosinski's own experiences. There are also scenes of a young university student in an Eastern European university trying desperately to coexist with the collectivization which he detests, reminiscent of Kosinski's stories about himself attending Polish or Russian universities as well as scenes in which a young university student defects to the United States and tries desperately to make a living and at the same time learn the language of his new country. Characters like the protagonist of these scenes, and the scenic backdrop itself, recur in most of Kosinski's novels.

At least six scenes deal with the motif of revenge, also a staple of all of Kosinski's fiction.[5]

Fifteen of the scenes in the novel involve the exposition or analysis of what I shall call examples of "kinky sex."[6] Such scenes of course are a hallmark of all Kosinski novels. And indeed, the italicized dialogues, which I am treating separately, constitute thirteen more kinky-sex examples.

The Autobiographical Episodes

The "autobiographical" episodes which seem like parts of *The Painted Bird,* or which deal with the protagonist as a university student in Eastern Europe, are more interesting, and more discussable, under the other types: of revenge or kinky sex. But the episodes of one series, the longest connected series of episodes in the book (III: 8; IV:1, 2, 3, 4, 5), gain a special interest as possibly being documents of Kosinski's experiences at that moment when he was beginning to develop a new life in America. In the first of them we see the protagonist, twenty-four years old, in a plane which will take him to America, where he is going to defect. All his past is behind him, all his uncertain future ahead of him. He wishes the plane could simply stop in midair.

He arrives in America with his suitcases full of dictionaries, but no money. He sells film in order to get money for food. When that is gone, he steals food. He can speak no English at all.

He gets a job chipping paint at a wage well below the legal minimum, but other immigrants fight with him, so he is fired.

He gets a truckdriving job. At first he is terrified driving the huge truck through narrow congested downtown streets, but soon becomes fantastically expert. A black racketeer is so impressed with his driving, he hires him as a chauffeur. When the racketeer is negotiating with other gang leaders, they do their discussing while he has his chauffeur—the protagonist—drive them around. The protagonist, under his orders, drives at great speed, constantly narrowly missing other cars or obstacles. The other racketeers do not like to admit they are frightened, but in fact are so distracted the protagonist's employer makes very good deals with them.

He is sponsored by his employer at "knock off," a very dangerous competition played with fast cars on city streets. He wins all bets, but one day someone is killed in a contest.

These very interesting episodes do not seem to take part in what I will suggest are the major movements of the novel, but certainly typify Kosinski's penchant for inserting into his novels materials that we suspect to be directly autobiographical.

The Revenge Motif

I: 12, and III: 7 both seem to derive from *The Painted Bird*. Both have a revenge motif. The orphaned boy (I: 12) is maltreated by everyone in the village. One day a child dies from mushroom poisoning and when the boy sees the mourning of the parents he realizes to what excess the peasants love their children. Then he sees a cow die in agony. The peasants think it must have swallowed a fishhook or piece of broken glass. The boy is savagely beaten one day and begins saving abandoned fishhooks and shards of glass. The village children begin dying in terrible agony.

The rhythm of the scene is rather typical of Kosinski. First, we are shown how revenge could be accomplished if we wanted to revenge ourselves on someone. Then, almost providentially, the others do something to the protagonist to justify his revenge. The impulse for revenge seems to come before the offensive action that will require the revenge. I do not believe what I am observing here is something Kosinski intends. I believe it is simply the way he constructs his scene. But it gives the frequent revenge scenes in Kosinski's novels a special quality of distastefulness, sometimes, as if the protagonist willed his affronts, just to justify to himself performing the act of revenge.

In III: 7 we see another kind of revenge scene. It is after the war, and the boy is sleeping in an abandoned factory. The aged night watchman does not pose a threat to him, as he walks his rounds outside the

building, but merely by being there night after night he irritates the
boy. The boy lines up several old bottles by a high window, and begins
throwing them at the old man. The man remains in the line of fire,
refusing to back off, until a bottle kills him. The boy later reads in a
paper the old man had been watchman until the factory closed years
before, and he refused to leave the position, even after his job no longer
existed. He had served a long jail term once for deserting from the army
during the war.

Really, the story is about the old man, who must have blamed
himself even more than society had blamed him for deserting his post
once in a fit of cowardice. He had refused to stop guarding the
factory—even when his presence was no longer required—no doubt out
of a compact he had made with himself never again to desert a post. And
at last he has this second chance to stand still under fire, and indeed dies
in the line of duty. A nice little story, but how typical of Kosinski to tell
it from the standpoint of the person who murders him, and, in fact, to
make his murderer the protagonist through whose eyes we see the story,
the protagonist we had identified with.

It might simply be a question of narrative economy. The protagonist
has to be in the story anyway, so rather than creating another character
to actuate the plot, it might as well be the protagonist. But this
happens so frequently in Kosinski's writing that we must suspect
intention, an attempt to incriminate the protagonist, and through
him, us who have identified with him. Other examples would be the
fact that, in the famous scene of the bird being painted so that the other
birds will turn on it, it is the boy, in *The Painted Bird,* who catches the
bird. Or the scene in *The Future Is Ours, Comrade,* which I described in
Chapter 2, where because the protagonist, presumably Kosinski himself, has a love affair with a girl, she is punished by her collective and
sent off to a remote province. The recurring pattern is that the protagonist is the operative factor in the harm that comes to the other
character, and yet the protagonist is never himself harmed, or afterwards affected.

There is a scene, I: 10, which foreshadows similar scenes in later
Kosinski novels, where the protagonist revenges not a personal affront,
but a wrong done to others, carrying the revenge theme up a notch, to
become a sort of "scourge of God." As a soldier out on maneuvers, he

observes another soldier shooting from a distance a man and a woman, apparently just for the fun of it. The paper reports two people killed by stray bullets. The next day several in the regiment are killed when they drive into an artillery range that "someone in the regiment may have removed the warning sign from" (33).[7] The implication is that the protagonist himself removed it.

Kinky Sex

In II: 6 he is editor of the student newspaper, and so he is able to give a high post to a pretty girl, but he still cannot get anywhere with the girl. He notices that, while she ignores all his advances, she seems to spend all her time watching and admiring herself. One day when she is out of the room of her apartment, he looks through her drawers and finds some nude photographs she seems to have taken of herself. He takes these, and whenever he has friends over at his house, he leaves the photographs in places where they will be sure to discover them. The rumor is soon going around that he is sleeping with the girl. One day the girl commits suicide. It is immediately assumed that he seduced her, made her pregnant, and then abandoned her. He receives numerous anonymous notes accusing him. His friends ostracize him. At the funeral he sees other students pointing him out to the girl's father. The old man comes over and spits in his eye.

Typically, no comment is made by Kosinski. The young man had in fact had nothing whatever to do with the girl's suicide, which probably was related in some way to her neurotic self-absorption. What is his feeling looking in the face of her father—guilt that he had wanted to be the person the father blames? Embarrassment at being in this fix where he is innocent, but in no position to convince anyone of his innocence? Proud of the reputation he has formed as a cruel seducer?[8]

In I: 17 he is a photographer assigned to take photographs at a home for the aged, making them look serene and beautiful. He finds this difficult to do, as they are hideous and drooling and senile, dying bitterly before his eyes. Then he sees a young nurse and is immediately attracted to her. "I did not care whether or not she was beautiful; it was enough that she was clean and healthy. I desperately wanted to reassure myself that I had nothing in common with the inmates" (50). He finds out she had come as a psychology student wanting to study, briefly, the aged and retarded, and now has stayed on for three years. He gets the nurse to help him in his photographic task. As they go about, the senile and doddering old men paw at her and make suggestive comments. She accepts it impassively: "She told me it was only to be expected" (50). When the protagonist also touches her at every excuse, she also impassively endures it, but gives him no other sign of attention. "To her, perhaps, there was nothing different or unusual about me. I might have been just another patient, merely a little younger, a little less decrepit than the others. I began finding certain points of similarity between myself and the inmates. Nor could I avoid the realization that one day I would become what they were now" (51).

Then he surprised her in the act of making love to "the furry body of a creature with a human head, pawlike hands, and the short, barrel-chested trunk of an ape" (53). The creature races off yelping, and dives into a crib. The creature, he notices, is human.

Again, no comment by Kosinski, but we wonder if for the nurse, also, her lover did not need to be beautiful, only healthy, and in this case, because unable to develop, also ageless, as though its inability to grow up has spared it from our common decay and has spared the nurse from being reminded of it, even with all the death around her.

III: 2 seems to have a European, perhaps an Eastern European, setting. The protagonist finds a demented woman kept in a cage in a barn, where the men of the village go to take advantage of her. He is briefly tempted by the situation "where one could become completely oneself with another human being." But it is not quite kinky enough: "What I required, however, was the other's recognition of this: the woman in the cage could not acknowledge me" (86). So instead he brings the police, who arrest the farmer who had kept her, and put the woman in an asylum. The church is very much the center of the village. Months later, the protagonist comes back and challenges the priest, saying he must have known what was going on, because the men in the village must have confessed to him that they were resorting to her. Why didn't he do anything about it? Why didn't he release the woman himself? (One does not sense, on the protagonist's part, moral outrage, but merely psychological curiosity.)

The priest has no answer; once more, typically, Kosinski has made the protagonist the moving or catalyzing force in the action.[9]

The protagonist, III: 5, is obsessed by a girl who works in his office, but she refuses to go out with him. He goes to the extreme of having a friend of his make the girl his mistress, and then the friend demands of the girl, as a proof of her love for him, that she submit to another man, while she is blindfolded. That is the protagonist's chance. He comes to her where his friend has left her, naked and blindfolded. At first she is very unwilling, but then she responds ardently to his caresses. But as soon as he leaves he can no longer connect the passionate, naked, blindfolded girl with the clothed, indifferent girl he still must see every day at the office, who, of course, does not realize she is his lover. He has had his will of her, but she does not know it, and so the experience has been spoiled for him. As in III: 2 above, what he requires is the other's "recognition" of his mastery, a theme that is carried out to its fullest in the italicized dialogues.

The Italicized Dialogues

The theme is an important one in Kosinski's writing. Just as the collectivized society tyrannizes over the individual, tries to make the individual become only what the collective perceives him as being, tries to make him perceive himself through its eyes, so, too, do individuals in their personal relationships attempt to make others become what the first individual perceives them to be, while at the same time preserving his own identity. In terms reminiscent of Jean Paul Sartre's Existentialist psychology, Kosinski suggests that in a relationship between a man and a woman, each attempts to remain the subject, while making of the other an object. The dialogues begin with a discussion of circumcision, asking if that first sexual offense against the defenseless infant does not rob it of something essential. Next they discuss his (i.e., the man in the dialogue's) inability to tolerate the thought that she might be thinking of someone else, might, in other words, still be capable of life apart from him. Perhaps as a test of this, he sends her to get a massage. She is surprised that it is to a masseur instead of a masseuse that he has sent her. The man massages her sexually, which she allows, because "they were not his hands any more . . . they were your hands" (43). He has her followed once while he is gone, and discovers she has taken a lover. "I had to find out whether I could still be interested in someone else. . . . I felt I had an obligation to know myself better—apart from the self you have brought me to know" (44).

She is trying to decide if she has chosen the protagonist as a lover, or if he has already influenced her so much she is no longer capable of choice and has simply become an object of his mind. But she perhaps begins to feel drained by him (53), and we have, for what may be an extreme comparison to her situation, the unitalicized episode of the protagonist out walking with his girl friend (a different girl, from an earlier period of his life) when they are attacked, and the girl is brutally gang-raped. He tries to go on thinking of her the same way, but she has become distanced from him, a complete object. He finds himself experimenting with her. He gets her to take a lesbian lover so he can watch, encourages her to become an alcoholic, at last takes her to a party and turns her over to all his male friends and leaves (I: 19).

This vignette suggests that the subject-object relationship is destructive, and yet there does not appear to be much choice. If one is not the destroyer, then one must submit and become the destroyed object. Other vignettes support such a conclusion. It is not clear, however, that the relationship between the italicized couple is quite so desperate. They seem to be trying to work out their relationship, and to work it out with considerable honesty.

The protagonist suggests to the woman at one point in the dialogues that she must try to preserve the idea of herself during their love-making: "Lovers are not snails; they don't have to protrude from their shells and meet each other halfway. Meet me within your own self. . . . I want you, you alone. But beyond you and me together, I see myself in our love-making. It is this vision of myself as your lover I wish to retain and make more real." She asks, "But you do want me for what I am, apart from you, don't you?" and he replies, "I don't know you apart from myself" (131; italics removed).

But it is not easy, perhaps not even very desirable, for one to meet another within one's own self, for in one of the early episodes (I: 5) the protagonist (after visiting an aquarium, where he sees an obviously very symbolical octopus eating its own body) finds himself impotent with an exciting woman. In frustration he goes with a woman he meets on the streets, who handles him just as he would handle himself, and then he suddenly sees it is a man dressed as a woman. "All we could do," he concludes, "is exist for each other as a reminder of the self" (24).

It seems very little, but what are the alternatives? To tyrannize over the loved object? Or worse, to submit and become that selfless object?

Kosinski's Purest Novel

If we come back to *Steps* after reading all of Kosinski's other books, we cannot escape the feeling that we are looking at bits and pieces of several of his novels, particularly *Cockpit* and *Blind Date*, novels Kosinski was not to write for several years after writing *Steps*. And we are not looking at rejected scenes (except for one or two scenes that may have been cut out of *The Painted Bird*), for these scenes equal in complexity and impact many of the best scenes of the later novels. What is different in *Steps* is the lack—except in a few places—of continuity, the lack of a protagonist who is dependably the same protagonist throughout. Kosinski, in *Steps*, has radically denied "plot," and placed all his emphasis, and all the reader's attention, on the individual incident.

Let me quote again what he told Gail Sheehy about "incident."

An incident is simply a moment of life's drama of which we are aware as it takes place. This awareness and the intensity of it decides, in my view, whether our life is nothing but a barely perceived existence, or meaningful living. To intensify life, one must not only recognize each moment as an incident full of drama, but, above all, oneself as its chief protagonist. To bypass that moment, to dilute it in the gray everydayness, is to waste the most precious ingredient of living: the awareness of being alive. That's why in my fiction I stress incident, as opposed, let's say, to a popular culture, which stresses a plot. Plot is an artificially imposed notion of preordained "destiny" that usually dismisses the importance of life's each moment. Yet, that moment carries the essence of our life.[10]

Now if I am correct that Kosinski's intention in the "plotless" structure of *Steps* is to make us give our full attention to each episode as it happens, as he suggests we should give our full attention to each episode in our actual lives, with ourselves as chief protagonist, I wonder if he then intends us to identify ourselves with the protagonist of the incidents in his novel? He is quite often an unattractive person, and Kosinski has explicitly condemned him: he has described him as a person "always in step with the culture, unable to walk any other staircase." But he also says that the novel's loose structure is designed to be filled in with "the reader's 'own formulated experiences.'"[11]

Are we then to identify with the protagonist at the same moment that Kosinski is criticizing him for his conformity to the collective values of his culture? Is the novel an attack upon us, the complacent readers? Does he mean to awaken us, through our dwelling on the incident, to the true values of life? Interviewer: "Your intent, then, is subversive. You want to involve, to implicate the reader via his own imagination." Kosinski: "I guess I do. Once he is implicated he is an accomplice, he is provoked, he is involved, he is purged. That's why I won't give him moral guidelines. The reader must ask himself questions. Was it his curiosity that dragged him into the midst of my story, or was it recognition, his complicity?"[12]

How do we react to Kosinski's challenge? We are in fact, most of us, pretty passive readers, titillated, perhaps, by erotic parts of the novel, excited by action, suspended by suspense—but do we morally implicate ourselves in the actions? I have discussed, in Chapter 3, the revenge motif running through all of Kosinski's work, and I have explained why it appears to me that Kosinski is morally approving of revenge, and works, in his novels (not always successfully), to make it an acceptable, necessary action. The central moral concern in *Steps,* however, is not revenge, but the relationship between human beings. The first-person narrator, whom we tend to relate to, struggles to form a relationship with a woman that will not be annihilating for either of them. The suggestion is made throughout the book that no other kind of relationship is possible except the dominating object-creating one, but we suspect that cannot be Kosinski's point. For whatever it is worth as evidence of Kosinski's intention, we can go outside the novel to note that Kosinski himself does not seem to have any problem forming close and long-lasting relationships with others. So perhaps we can assume that he is critical of his protagonist and make some sense of his statement that the protagonist is a person "always in step with the culture, unable to walk any other staircase."

If Kosinski's two intentions for his novels are that they present moral dilemmas without comment, putting the burden of moral decision on the reader, and that they push the incident forward in our consciousness by rejecting plot, then we are entitled to call *Steps* Kosinski's purest novel, or at any rate the purest working out of his aesthetic intention. His moral commentary is so muffled or absent that it is difficult to know in what way he intends us to respond to the incidents in *Steps,* and so, as in actual life situations, in reading the book we are thrown on our own resources.

Structurally, also, *Steps* is and must remain Kosinski's purest work.[13] In his first novel, *The Painted Bird,* Kosinski was telling the story of a young boy, and though many of the events that befall him could be presented to us in almost any order, the novel is not entirely episodic, because, as I have tried to suggest in Chapter 3, a story about a young boy is almost willy-nilly "plotted" or organized around the theme of education. A young boy cannot merely experience: he learns by experience; he begins from innocence, but cannot maintain it (unless, like Chance in *Being There*—see Chapter 5—he is simple), and the movement from innocence to "experience" forms a plot.

With *Steps* Kosinski was cut loose from plot, and also cut loose from the obviously thematic ordering, and the necessity of sticking to facts, of the first two nonfiction books. In this respect, *Steps* represents the most extreme statement of his aesthetic possible. But by its nature, he could only write with such purity once, for the reason that to write a second book the same way would merely be to write *Steps* over again, a continuation of the first book, which has really no beginning or end. Indeed the problem he has faced, sometimes more, sometimes less successfully, in the novels to follow *Steps* is that of how to stick to his episode-centered method and yet seem to be writing different books.

The Art of the Self

The purity with which Kosinski refrained from giving us any moral guidelines in *Steps* has been somewhat diminished by his subsequently publishing a long essay, *The Art of the Self: Essays à Propos "Steps."* It is his second Scientia-Factum booklet. As with *Notes of the Author,* these notes were originally published without Kosinski's permission, and he had to publish them himself to prevent them from going into the public domain. They were part of his correspondence with his Dutch-language publishers, which he utilized in a seminar at Wesleyan, and which his students published in the school newspaper.

Kosinski stresses that the essay is not entitled essays "about" *Steps,* but rather, essays "à propos" *Steps.* Many of the notes take off in wide tangents from the novel and are not intended as a reading guide to the novel, and Kosinski feels uneasy when the essay is used for that purpose. Nevertheless it is a long statement of Kosinski's philosophy and aesthetic, and, even keeping Kosinski's caveats in mind, its statements seem to have useful application not only to *Steps* but to other Kosinski novels.

At least one objective of the essay must have been to connect *Steps* with serious art of all time, for in various of the brief statements Kosinski seems to parallel his novel with Greek, Italian, neoclassical French, Renaissance, and modern drama, with montage in film, with action painting and op art, with works of Sophocles, Shakespeare, Camus, Sartre, Günter Grass, de Sade, Wilde, Genet, Bosch, Dostoevski, and even prereligious ritual.

A second, much more important objective, however, is to suggest some of the philosophical underpinnings of his novel. The discussion is difficult, but worth looking at because of the light it casts on a good deal of Kosinski's writing.

Subject and Object

As would be expected, the *Essays* present a philosophy having to do with the preservation of the self in a world which seeks to destroy or subvert it. In terms which Kosinski himself suggests he took from Sartre, he speaks of the self as a "subject" which maintains its integrity by making all else into an "object" (34).[14] The narrator, or protagonist, of *Steps* has two goals, (1) to find out who he is, what self is his, and (2) to avoid the loss or dilution of that self into some larger whole.

Defining the self is difficult in the first place because the self is so protean. "The leit-motif of *Steps* is metamorphosis. The protagonist changes his external appearance and plays all the characters. He is a tourist, archeological assistant, skiing instructor, a deserting soldier, a sniper in the army, a photographer . . . (17).[15] The narrator, Kosinski tells us, "creates each situation rather than being a reactor in it" (16). He creates the situations to see what new "*I*'s" will come out of them, trying to discover his ephemeral self. "He seeks unforeseen situations to take the place of his predictable imagination" (16).

The imagination, then—in addition to such standard threats as society, religion, and other collective institutions—can be one of the many enemies of selfhood, because imagination comes between the narrator and "reality," and it is only in reality that the self exists: "for the narrator reality becomes a prerequisite of consciousness of the self" (17). Partly this is because the imagination can tie us to past memory, and reality exists only in the present instant.[16] Here is one of the reasons Kosinski rejects plot in his fictions: it is a falsification of reality. Indeed, even the episode is suspect, since it contains some cause-and-effect relations, which, of course, dilute the reality of the present instant by making it appear that the present was caused by the past, rather than existing autonomously. "We seem to perceive reality in episodes, in groups of organized 'acknowledgments.' The episode—in its extension the plot, is . . . the way meaning is conveyed to the reader. . . . Modern art attempts to break down the blocks of perceptions in order to create a reality of pure perception, reality before it is formed into episodes. It objects to the imposing on the present a form of the past, an episode, since it claims that original perception precedes all forms" (16).

Such a philosophy has repercussions on personal relationships. In order to preserve his *I* the protagonist seemingly must dominate or control the rest of his universe, must make himself *subject* and the rest of the world, including other people, *object*. He makes another person into an object by imposing his imagination—that is, his past—on that person. The dominance is destructive: once that person becomes an object of his past, the person no longer exists in the reality of the present.

The narrator's relationships with others in *Steps* are certainly manipulative, aggressive, and destructive: "The only truly satisfying relationship, then, is one of growing domination, one in which [the narrator's] experience—a certain form of the past—can be projected onto the other person. Until this hold is gained (assuming that the 'prey' has some awareness of the protagonist's purpose), the 'prey' maintains some superiority over the protagonist and remains his rival" (20).

So far it would seem that the protagonist of *Steps* is almost admirable, valiantly preserving his selfhood against all hazards. But I suggested in my analysis of the novel that we are to be critical of the protagonist, because there exist in the world possibilities for human relationships that are not destructive. Kosinski's attitude toward his protagonist, as evidenced in *The Art of the Self*, is almost as protean as the protagonist himself is, but in one passage, at least, he offers support for my reading of the novel: he is discussing the episode (I:3) in which the healthy ski instructors make love to the moribund patients in the sanitorium as a relationship of subject/sadists and object/masochists. The ski instructors, he tells us, "understood little of 'love,' which, one supposes, is the attempt to be simultaneously subject and object, and is the willing relinquishment of the single subject to a new subject created from two single ones, each subject enhanced into one heightened self" (31).

The Final Episode

The final episode in *Steps* is, if possible, even more puzzling and ambiguous than many episodes preceding it. Suddenly the point of view shifts to the woman. The *I* narrator of the episodes, who is also the *he* of the italic dialogues, abruptly vanishes, after making a final statement to her in the next-to-last episode:

When I'm gone, I'll be for you just another memory descending upon you uninvited, stirring up your thoughts, confusing your feelings. And then you'll recognize yourself in this woman. (146; italics removed)

He has left her. She goes down to the beach, undresses, enters the water, and begins swimming. "A small rotten leaf brushed against her lips. Taking a deep breath, she dove beneath the surface. On the bottom a shadow glided over the seaweed, lending life and motion to the ocean floor. She looked up through the water to find its source and caught sight of the tiny leaf that had touched her before (147–48).

Thus the novel concludes. Now, to show how difficult Kosinski can be, and how tentatively we should interpret him, I read the final passage this way: I know that Kosinski was severely traumatized by water as a child, when he was pushed under the ice of a river. Death or threat of death by water, by murder or suicide, recurs in many of his novels. Therefore, when the final sentence of *Steps* shows the woman diving under the water after being deserted by her man, I assumed she was committing suicide. But, taking a passage from the essay *The Art of the Self,* I read the suicide as, at least symbolically, a positive act, her freeing herself from his domination, and asserting the primacy of her own self, for Kosinski wrote that "Suicide is an act of the present. In performing it a man chooses to escape from his future and from his past, thus overcoming the knowledge that he will die. By suicide, he takes over a natural function. To die in nature's time is to accede to a denial of man's dignity: to die in one's own time is to affirm that dignity" (23).

Kosinski, who agrees with me that the ending is meant to be positive, disagrees with me in everything else. First of all, he tells me, he did not intend the passage on suicide in *The Art of the Self* to have anything at all to do with the novel *Steps.* Second, he did not intend that final deep dive to imply suicide. "I have not intended to portray or even to insinuate a suicide here. Indeed, I see it as the heroine's reaffirmation of her independence from the "steps" she has "walked" till now. Taking a deep breath (a sign of control, of life, isn't it?) she dives beneath the surface (merely beneath the surface—does not throw herself into the depths!)—she then *looks up* to find the source of the shadow and finds it above (read behind) her: nothing more than a tiny leaf that *had* touched her *before*—but does not touch her anymore. Hence, she is free, her past a source of perceivable impression—but no more than a shadow *lending life and motion!*"

Chapter Five
Being There and The Devil Tree

Kosinski's next two novels are in some respects untypical of the rest of his work, but bear certain resemblances to each other, so that perhaps they can be conveniently examined in the same chapter.

Being There, his third novel (a novella, really, less than 23,000 words long), was the first of his books to be dedicated to "Katherina v. F.," as every subsequent work has been. Though Kosinski's style in previous novels was stripped and spare, in *Being There* there is even further refinement. The work is written—though it is detailed and graphic enough in certain sexual scenes—with the simplicity of a parable or moral allegory, which in many respects it is.

Being There

Chance has lived all his life inside a walled garden, which he tends devotedly. He has little idea who his parents were. The garden belongs to the Old Man, who has taken him in to tend it. The Old Man has told him his brain is damaged. If he leaves the garden, he will be put into an insane asylum. He has had no education. He has never learned to read and write. All he knows of life is the garden, and what he sees on television, which he watches constantly. An occasional maintenance man about the house tries to teach him about sex, but he does not really get the point, and besides, he evidently is completely impotent. He is, however, tall, handsome, soft-spoken.

The Old Man dies. Since there is no record of Chance's having any connection with the house, the executors turn him out on the street. He has packed and taken with him the expensive hand-tailored suits the Old Man had cast off and given him. Their 1920s styling is back in vogue.

He walks innocently out into the street and is at once struck, and slightly injured, by a chauffeur-driven limousine. The woman riding in it, seeing that he is handsome and expensively dressed, takes him to her mansion to recover. There are many doctors in the house since her husband, decades her senior, is dying. He is a fabulously wealthy financier. When he talks to Chance, Chance answers everything in terms of the garden—which is practically all he knows—and in every situation in which he is placed, patterns his behavior on some similar scene he has watched on television.

His comments on the garden are taken for brilliant metaphorical statements on the economy. The President of the United States visits the financier, talks to Chance, and that night quotes one of his gardening statements in a major address. Suddenly everyone is talking about Chance, he is on talk shows and sought after by all the media, his favor is curried by the Russian ambassador. The financier's wife is madly in love with him—with the sanction of her husband, who wants to see her in good hands after his death. Because of his actually blank surface, he can be everything to everyone. By the end of this brief novel, he is being considered for high office, having the marvelous advantage of looking good on television and having no past to embarrass him.

The Biblical Allegory

The obvious biblical parallels of the first few pages of the novel push the reader toward interpreting the action allegorically. It begins on Sunday, traditionally the day on which the creation of the world was complete. Chance is in the garden, tending the plants. He lives in peace, ignorant of what life may exist on the streets outside the walls of the garden, and almost as ignorant of what goes on inside the house where the Old Man lives. His helpmeet is the black maid, Louise, who brings him his meals, but otherwise has little to do with him. No one else is ever to see him, except the Old Man, who might occasionally walk in the garden. He has been instructed never to leave the garden, but always to tend it. The maintenance man, a tempting devil, occasionally comes in the garden, however, and shows Chance pictures of naked men and women handling each other, but Chance can make nothing of them. He thinks to ask Louise about them, but never does. Then Louise gets "sick" and leaves. Does this unexplained sickness represent her pregnancy by the maintenance man? Or does it represent the mortality of those who, unlike Chance, live within the flow of time? Chance, at any rate, remains in pristine innocence.

But one day the new maid calls him to come see the Old Man: "The Old Man was propped against the stiff pillows and seemed poised intently, as if he were listening to a trickling whisper in the gutter. His shoulders sloped down at sharp angles, and his head, like a heavy fruit on a twig, hung down to one side (9).[1]

The "fruit" no doubt is the knowledge of death, though in fact it makes little impression on Chance, who wanders off to watch TV. But it is enough to have him thrown out of the garden for good the next day by the executors of the estate.

The first person he meets outside the garden is the woman whose limousine accidentally strikes him. Her name is Elizabeth Eve, called by her friends EE. The name Eve (primal innocence) is obvious enough in the allegorical scheme. Perhaps Elizabeth suggests the "virgin queen;" for it is difficult to imagine any sexual congress between her and her ancient dying husband, who, because of his great wealth and influence, his moribund state, and his caretaker relationship with her, parallels exactly Chance's Old Man. They are both God figures, and this second one, EE's husband, tries his best to throw Chance and Eve together. For her part, much less innocent than Chance, she does all she can to seduce him, to open his eyes to good and evil.

While the presence of the allegory is for the most part obvious, the question of what exactly to make of it is not.[2] Is it significant that the two God figures are dead or dying? The universe seems to be one in which God is prime mover, setting the machinery going, then leaving the people on their own. More than that, chance dominates this mechanistic world. "His name was Chance," the Old Man tells the protagonist, because he had been born by chance" (8). We know this is Kosinski's own view of the universe, an arena where nothing is planned, nothing preordained, nothing here "for a purpose," but all is the chance mutation of the chance events that impinge upon it, as suggested in the book *Chance and Necessity,* written by Kosinski's good friend Jacques Monod.

The world of chance is an existential world where man makes his own meaning, or else lives his life pointlessly and dies. On the first page of the novel Kosinski contrasted plants with people. In physical ways, they were alike: "they needed care to live, to survive their diseases, and to die peacefully. Yet plants were different from people. No plant is able to think about itself or able to know itself; there is no mirror in which the plant can recognize its face; no plant can do anything intentionally; it cannot help growing, and its growth has no meaning, since a plant cannot reason or dream" (3–4).

A person can reason or dream, but may not; may fail of this activity and live meaninglessly and die, not having lived as a human being. Chance lives, almost like his plants, without reflection, without curiosity. But this, we are told, is because his brain has been damaged. We are not told what has damaged his brain, or in what way it is damaged, but we do know that he spends almost all of his time watching television, and his only notion of life, besides his physical awareness of growth and decay, is what is given to him through television.

Television as the Enemy of Experience

Being There contains the first statements in novel form of the theme Kosinski himself is quite outspoken on in essays and interviews. Television, through the seductiveness of its easy, mindless images, destroys both our physical response to the actual world before us and our imaginative ability to respond and give moral value to actions in the real world. It destroys our life by making us settle for a secondhand life at one remove, and it destroys meaning in our life by prepackaging all moral issues and feeding them to us on an assembly line.

To begin with, in the world of *Being There,* no one *is* there for other characters until he has been recorded in some mechanical fashion. The executors of the Old Man's estate pore through all his papers, but can find no record of Chance existing there. Therefore, to their minds, he does not exist. He cannot *prove* he exists. " 'But,' said Chance, 'you have me. I am here. What more proof do you need?' " (22).

Well, they need a birth certificate, a shot record, a tax statement, anything. . . .

Indeed, Chance had already begun to feel his own insubstantiality: "As long as one didn't look at people, they did not exist. They began to exist, as on TV, when one turned one's eyes on them. Only then could they stay in one's mind before being erased by new images. The same was true of him. By looking at him, others could make him be clear, could open him up and unfold him; not to be seen was to blur and fade out" (14).

In such a solipsistic world, the world of the mechanically produced visual image, Chance had a peculiar advantage. Because he had grown up looking at TV and nothing else, in his appearance and manner he had come to resemble a bland TV image himself, and people looking at him immediately recognize the image and respond to it. He is "manly; well-groomed; beautiful voice; sort of a cross between Ted Kennedy and Cary Grant" (70). But the cost to him is that, as he recognizes himself, he exists only as an object for the others. They fill his empty shell with their own dreams and longings, not knowing that he is actually incapable of giving them the substance. In one scene a homosexual and in another scene Elizabeth Eve herself have with Chance what they think to be the most rewarding and fully realized sexual relations they have ever had with anyone, not realizing that, in the presence of his passive incomprehension, their activity has been purely onanistic.

By the end of the novel, the boys in the smoke-filled back rooms are grooming him for high office. After all, he "has no background! And so he's not and cannot be objectionable to anyone! He's personable, well-spoken, and he comes across well on TV! And, as far as his thinking goes, he appears to be one of us" (139).

What more could anyone ask of a political leader? The novel seems to be suggesting that such a character could easily find himself, at last, in the oval office, with the power to destroy the world one button away. We would have put him there through our television-induced inability to distinguish between actual substance and empty image.[3]

Autobiographical Elements in *Being There*

"'That reminds me,' Mr. Kosinski went on, 'of a classic question I was asked the other day by one of the out-of-town reviewers. "Would this book," he asked me, 'like your other two books, be autobiographical' Mr. Kosinski smiled. 'The best I could do was tell him that to some degree we are all retarded. And one day, of course, we all will be retarded together.'"[4]

In fact, many readers criticized *Being There,* and Kosinski's next novel, *The Devil Tree,* for not being sufficiently autobiographical, for taking him out of the realm of his personal experience (in Eastern Europe during the war, and after the war in a collectivized society, and in New York as an impoverished immigrant) and dealing instead with the life of the incredibly wealthy, of which he knew nothing.

As we have seen, however, his experience of life among the very rich was considerable.[5] The dying old financier and his youthful wife, Elizabeth Eve, might have been inspired by the industrialist Weir and his widow Mary, who became Kosinski's wife.[6] They are, of course, gently satirized in *Being There,* as is everyone else in that satirical parable.

The Devil Tree

The Devil Tree, Kosinski's fourth novel, similarly utilizes in its background Kosinski's experiences living among the very wealthy. The father of the protagonist, Jonathan Whalen, is again a portrayal of industrialist Weir. Whalen himself, the youthful hippie protagonist, scion of an enormously wealthy family, is such a young man as Kosinski taught at Yale, Princeton, and Wesleyan.[7] And again as in *Being There,* the protagonist is a victim of the mechanized society that imprisons men's minds as surely as the most openly totalitarian regime.

Whalen, the young protagonist, is one week away from his twenty-first birthday, dressed like a bum, and carrying no identification ("Why should I? . . . There's no law in this country that says I have to carry identification papers" (7),[8] when the police pick him up to check him out as a suspicious character. What they find out is that he is heir to one of the largest fortunes in the country, that interest on money held in trust for him is paying him $25,000 a month, and that next week the principal becomes his.

As the story unfolds, in typical Kosinski fashion through a series of brief, sharply focused vignettes, we discover that Whalen, apart from the staggering wealth that allows him to do or have anything he wants and gives him power over others' lives, is essentially like any number of young people of the 1960s and early 1970s. He has drifted through India, Burma, Africa; he has tried every drug, and at one point needed treatment for a serious addiction problem. He goes to astrologers, encounter-group therapy, and has an endless, on-again-off-again lacerating sexual relationship with Karen, a girl who similarly has experimented with every kind of sex, and from month to month is passionately but superficially into feminism or whatever the next *ism* is.

But the freedom that Whalen's wealth gives him is not absolute. Spiritually, he is tied to the past that created him. Practically, he finds he has certain responsibilities. His father is dead; and now he, the heir, is nominally in charge of the vast business interests. He discovers, for instance, that the corporation has him followed everywhere—for his protection, of course. He might be kidnapped and endanger the business interests. And then he is subjected to tiresome meetings with boards of directors, who want some action, some decision from him. It turns out that the Howmets, old friends of the family, are largely responsible for his harrassment. They try to get Whalen away from his hippie ways and into the orbit of the business. They have Whalen join an influential Masonic order and begin grooming him for a responsible managerial position. In seeming gratitude, he invites them—taking them in his chartered jet—to a private retreat in East Africa, and there strands them on a remote reef, where the incoming tide will drown them.

It is his final attempt to deny his past roots, but the act does not seem to be sufficiently cathartic. He feels himself getting out of control. One day he hires a top coach to train him to be a world-class skier in an impossibly short time. Next we see him making love to some anonymous woman, then stopping, withdrawing, and beating her instead. Then we see him ill, recovering in some clinic in Switzerland. He gets up one night, leaves his room, stands at the edge of the lake, looking at the blinking lights on the far side. The novel ends at this point.

The Image of "the Devil Tree"

A note at the beginning of the novel explains the significance of the title. "The native calls the baobab 'the devil tree' because he claims that the devil, getting tangled in its branches, punished the tree by reversing it. To the native, the roots are branches now, and the branches are roots. To ensure that there would be no more baobabs, the devil destroyed all the young ones. That's why, the native says, there are only full-grown baobab trees left" (1).

The note serves very well as a symbolical formula for the novel. Whalen would like to reject his past (his roots), since that past, represented by the wealth amassed by his dead father, is based on ruthless exploitation of the poor and powerless. But his own power and freedom of action depend on that immoral wealth. In his quest to discover who he is himself, he must come to terms with that past (dig up his roots), but in so doing, will he bury himself (the branches)? Is the devil too firmly intermixed with every part of the tree ever to be extirpated without first destroying the young trees, the new generation, represented by Whalen?

Whalen's Quest for Identity

Who is Whalen? Our first view of him, in the opening pages of the novel, is both contradictory, and revealing. We see a young man, dressed like a hippie, with no living parents, no identification. He is a counterculture figure—except that he has $2,000 in his pocket. He tries to rent a helicopter to fly him over Manhattan. Because of his appearance he is met with suspicion. The pilot finally takes him—expecting every moment to be told to fly to Cuba—and has the police waiting to nab him the moment they land. "Put up your hands, fella" (6) is their first greeting, but when they check him out and discover how much wealth he represents, he immediately becomes "Mr. Whalen," and the police nervous and sycophantic. His sloppy clothing had fooled them, for their job obviously is to protect decent people like him from the suspicious people he had seemed to look like.

Which side is he on, then? He has just been on a helicopter ride over Manhattan. He asks the pilot how many people right this moment might be in helicopters looking down on Manhattan, and is told sixty. "Sixty people looking down at twelve million," said Whalen. "That's really something. For thirty dollars" (8). Money, in short, gives the few the privilege of looking down on the many.

Whalen, searching for himself, goes to an astrologer. "Saturn indicates feelings of separation and estrangement," he is told. "Having to leave familiar surroundings may well be a part of your destiny. Saturn also makes you hard on yourself. You are too impulsive, and have difficulty sticking to things. You must acquire patience and stability. You must protect your mental, physical and financial resources. You have great gifts: do not squander them" (14).

His father's valet also accuses him of squandering his gifts, suggesting that his travels, his drugs, his aimless life, are all evasions. But Whalen argues that "the freedom I have always desired has nothing to do with being able to travel or with surrendering responsibility; it means not being afraid, not disguising myself and not performing, not structuring my feelings to gain another's approval" (83). Yet when we see him in his encounter-group sessions, or his relationships with others, we see him adopt one role after another. Even his counterculture clothing is a pose, finally. He dresses thus so he can be "surrounded by people of his own kind" (9). Yet when the police, the guardians of the establishment culture, harass him, he quickly uses the power of his money to punish them for doing the job his money is paying them to do. "I see myself divided" (13), he says over and over again. "I have been . . . living in the present and refusing to examine my psyche or my past. But if I am to know myself, I will have to confront my contradictions and admit the impact of my childhood" (13). "When I play my father, I must speak in the voice that punishes me. Yet that condemning voice is also the voice which comforts me saying: 'Because you are my son, you are safe and better than others.' The roles overlap like a cover which protects a child but which may at the same time suffocate and destroy him" (35–36).

The Devil Tree and Steps

It may be useful, in pulling together the parts of so complex and fragmented a novel (it is written in 137 brief vignettes), to note how much it resembles in its design and in its philosophical bases Kosinski's earlier novel *Steps*.[9] It differs from *Steps* by very clearly having a single protagonist, who has a name, parents, a coherent past, and who is a young American. But it is like that novel in its dozens of brief, achronological dramatic incidents, in its glimpses of bizarre and often cruel and violent behavior throughout the world—usually in Europe and the United States—by which people try to control one another, and in its recurrent centering on the sexual relationship of the protagonist and the single woman who has been able to keep his attention beyond a brief affair.

To a lesser extent, but still like the protagonist of *Steps,* Whalen has several "selves." "My friends could never understand my ambivalence towards life. They thought I was continually drifting in and out of situations, trying to escape from myself and my family. They did not understand that I was pushing myself to extremes in order to discover my many selves" (31–32).

Again as in *Steps,* Whalen, while searching for his identity, constantly finds himself in power struggles with others to keep control of that identity, to be subject and make them his objects. At the same time he trembles on the edge of giving up some part of himself in order to enter into a love relationship, but finds the risks too severe.

And at the end of *The Devil Tree,* there is again the possibility of death by drowning, though this time it is the protagonist and not the woman who may contemplate suicide.

Whalen's Art of the Self

Because of the similarities between the two novels, it is helpful, in trying to sort out Kosinski's intentions in *The Devil Tree,* again to have reference to his booklet, *The Art of the Self.* (I refer the reader to my discussion of that essay in Chapter 4.

If the real self exists only in the present instant, then the past, which asserts a hold over the present, is an obstacle to be purged. Whalen's powerful father asserts the strongest hold from his past: "I explore my memories, trying to discover the substructure hidden beneath my past actions, searching for the link to connect them all . . . [my father's] unspoken words, which one day would explain everything" (25). "I still suffer from my father's rejection . . . yet . . . I deserve no punishment at all for being who I am" (35).

He cannot convince himself, however. Not only does he suffer from his dead father's disapproval because he did not follow in his father's footsteps, but he must also be racked by guilt that in many respects he does follow his father, never using his wealth for good ends, but only to assert his power and dominance over others: "I feel my old fear of violence returning. It began in early childhood when I lay in bed and listened to my father rage. . . . I remember how pleased I was that [my favorite biographies of heroes] never mentioned parents. These men seemed to have been born without fathers [i.e., without a past]; no wonder they had always been strong and powerful, able to mete out punishment whenever they pleased. They were born fathers" (36–37).

To overcome his self-hatred, he delves into his father's past, trying to neutralize it by getting to know it. He buys from a collector some of his father's letters, but finds the handwriting indecipherable. Then he picks up a black girl in a bar and takes her to the old family house, shut up and abandoned now. Making love to such a woman in his father's house is perhaps the greatest act of defiance he can think to make. He goes through all the memorabilia of his father in the house, and at last finds "the memories triggered no emotion" (133).

He is still not sufficiently purged, for when the police arrest him and the girl, assuming they are housebreakers, and he is punched by a policeman, he is not content to be himself—the desecrator of his father's memory—but rather makes known that he is his father's son, so that the frightened chief of police will punch the policeman in front of him in order to appease him.

Later in the novel he is still trying to learn about his father, and suddenly finds that "I have had a recurring physical sensation. It is as if the world were very sharply defined, but at the same time remote. Objects vibrate and quiver against me, but I cannot touch them" (157). The suggestion is that the past is still interfering with his apprehension of the present. In terms of *The Art of the Self,* his father has projected his past on Whalen, and made of Whalen an object, who is unable to live in the present moment.

Whalen will need to take some stronger measure to destroy that past, to liberate him to live in the present moment.

Whalen and Karen

In the meantime, as did the pair in the italicized dialogues in *Steps,* Whalen and Karen are jockeying for positions of dominance in their relationship. It is all lacerating and hopeless-seeming on the surface, and yet it appears that they both could let down their defenses enough for their relationship to achieve Kosinski's definition of love. That is, where neither strives to be subject at the expense of the other's becoming an object, but rather, there is "the attempt to be simultaneously subject and object," which involves "the willing relinquishment of the single subject to a new subject created from two single ones, each subject enhanced into one heightened self" (*The Art of the Self,* 31).

Karen "said she realized that I was right: there was a dependence between us that went beyond mere physical intimacy." But, she continues, "I feel the reverse of that fear I usually feel with others. I'm sure you'll accept the parts of me which are complex, but I'm not so sure about the parts that are ridiculously simple." He replies to her, "I had always wanted to conceal both portions of my own personality: the manipulative, malevolent adult who deceives and destroys: and the child who craves acceptance and love. . . . My worst terror has always been that I will seem helpless, that appearing childish I will again be judged in relation to my parents" (23).

He admits that "I am always afraid that some incident from my past will destroy other people's affection for me. . . . But with Karen I'm not so frightened" (31). "The possibility of becoming close to Karen is more exciting than anything else has ever been. I begin to feel that I could be loved for whatever I am, not for my actions or my appearance. Everything about me would be acceptable; everything would be a reflection buried within me that will surface as soon as I know I am completely loved" (32). But a moment later he vacillates: "Perhaps she will ridicule me for being naïve and banal. I regret having made myself so accessible" (33).

Karen says, "I tell myself that it's all right if I don't love you, but I can't stand your not loving me, because then I don't have any power over you. . . . I need your love. I'm terrified of being taken lightly" (67).

But they both remain wary. "My impulse is," Whalen says, "to remain elusive . . . but her own elusiveness makes this impossible: she intimidates me into talking frankly. . . . I am afraid that by our mutual silence we will both lose by default, with neither of us claiming victory over the other, and each going our separate way" (68).

The Destructive Act

Kosinski writes in *The Art of the Self*, "If sin is any act which prevents the self from functioning freely, the greatest sources of sin are those formerly protective agencies like society and religion. The original sense of 'creative' becomes completely reversed; now the only possible creative act, the independent act of choice and self-enhancement, seems to be the destructive act" (22).

Unable to escape from the domination of his past, unable to give himself freely in love to Karen, beginning to be haunted by death wishes and death fears, symbolizing his terror that his self is being taken from him, Whalen decides on a desperate action.[10] Mr. Howmet, an old friend of his father's, and standing now—with no encouragement from Whalen—*in loco parentis* to Whalen, tries to shake Whalen out of his childish counterculture pose and bring him into the sphere of the business, where he can take up his rightful place as director of the company.

Whalen pretends to accede, cuts his hair and wears a suit, and joins a Masonic order that Howmet insists on, then in seeming gratitude invites Howmet and his wife to the private resort where he murders them.

The Last Act

Whalen's reaction to his destructive act, the new creative act, is puzzling: he "felt energy flowing into him from outside as if he were a starving man being nourished from an unknown source. . . . Deep within himself he heard a child's laughter." So far it sounds promising, as if his action has brought power and freed the repressed child in him: "There were times when he lived on the far side of communicable thoughts and feelings." Again this sounds like what *The Art of the Self* advocates, the living so precisely in the present that "communicable thoughts and feelings" are impossible, because the communication already falsifies the present, makes it part of the past.[11] Yet, "he fought these moments, trying to tear off the membrane that seemed to enclose his mind and inhibit his will. But he was helpless and possessed, beyond self-control" (202).

So apparently the "energy" coming in from outside is what "possesses" him, and the possession has robbed him of control over his self, which is to say, has robbed him of his selfhood itself. The outside force, presumably, would be a combination of the powerful and dominating past and the equally powerful collective present.[12]

At any rate, after his act he flounders badly. We next see him hiring at great cost a top ski instructor, and asking him to train him from scratch to be a world-class downhill skiing champion in an impossibly short time. Here we have disquieting proof that he has not yet escaped his father, for we remember his talk with Anthony, his father's old valet. Anthony, after asking him what he meant to do with his life, had said, "I gather you don't plan to go into business. You're still quite young, and it would be a pity, a real pity, to waste yourself doing nothing or doing the wrong things. How about sports? Your father was not a bad golfer and a good swimmer and he was self taught. You can afford the best instructors, and in a short time you could develop real skill" (82).

Next we see him making love to the anonymous woman, but he is so remote from the present act of the moment that he must watch in the mirror as if witnessing his own actions from a distance. He still is not sufficiently asserting his sadistic dominance over her and begins beating her instead.

It is then he finds himself ill, presumably from a breakdown, and confined to a clinic in Geneva. He feels more and more distant from contact with reality: "Voices became abstractions, separated from the bodies of people moving around him. He sensed only surfaces. Forms became empty figures without gravity or weight" (207). One night his body refused to sleep. He rose, left the clinic and walked directly to the shore of the lake" (207).

The novel ends with Whalen standing there. Some critics have thought the ending hopeful, but I think we must conclude that he enters the water suicidally. We have the fact that Whalen's father died by drowning, the murder of the Howmets by drowning, and Whalen's earlier threat of drowning in the ice. We have the special threat always symbolized by water in Kosinski's books, perhaps growing out of his own traumatic experiences with water as a child.[13]

And so the only way the ending can be considered hopeful is in the philosophical sense: "to die in nature's time is to accede to a denial of man's dignity: to die in one's own time is to affirm that dignity" (*The Art of the Self,* 23). For Whalen, who, in Kosinski's words, was unable to "sustain his totality in a world of fragmenting values,"[14] perhaps the ultimate action of control over one's destiny was the single action remaining to him, a final nay-saying in a totalitarian state of the mind where everyone must say yes. Karen's girl friend had said, "Of all mammals, only a human being can say 'no.' A cow cannot imagine itself apart from the herd. That's why one cow is like any other. To say 'yes' is to follow the mass, to do what is commonly expected. To say 'no' is to deny the crowd, to be set apart, to reaffirm yourself" (193).

It is cold comfort, however, and, speaking sociologically, we must call *Being There* and *The Devil Tree* Kosinski's most pessimistic novels.

Autobiographical Elements in *The Devil Tree*

Earlier I quoted Kosinski as saying, "If anything, 'Being There' and 'Devil Tree' are more autobiographical than my other books." He was, perhaps, using a bit of polemical overstatement. Autobiographical elements, to be sure, exist in the two novels, but it is important to notice how differently employed they are in these novels contrasted with the others.

As in *Being There,* in *The Devil Tree* there is a character, Whalen's father, who obviously is based on steel magnate Ernest Weir, former husband of Kosinski's wife. Quite intriguing are two anecdotes about Whalen's father that—though I can find no confirmation for them elsewhere—have the ring of being true stories of Ernest Weir. In the first, "To prove his faith in American industry, my father insisted on shaving with an American-made steel blade for seven consecutive days." When Whalen's mother complained to the valet that his father's beard was a bit rough toward the end of the week, the valet began sneaking in a new blade. When Whalen's father discovered this one day, he instantly fired his faithful valet of twenty years (80–81). The second anecdote suggests that when Studebaker said it was going to produce a fiberglass, rather than a steel, car, Whalen's father used his immense power to force them into bankruptcy (82).

Another story, about Whalen's mother, we can confirm as true. A man tells Whalen he "had the good fortune to meet your mother about two years after your father's death." He finds her very attractive. "You might ask if I would have found her as attractive if she had been an ordinary office girl. But you see, she was not an ordinary office girl. . . . Just as an office girl is inseparable from her dreary job, your mother was inseparable from the elegant world through which she moved." They become lovers, and begin traveling together through that elegant world. "During our trips your mother never carried cash, so I took care of the tips when we left each place. Eventually I began carrying an attaché case filled with ones, fives and tens, ready for tipping." After two years, he had only two thousand dollars left from his savings of over ninety thousand (105–109). We know from Kosinski's own accounts that these were exactly his experiences in the years 1960–1968.

But what is important to note is the way in which these autobiographical elements are used in the two novels. They are used, essentially, to create the verisimilitude of the background, to create convincing portraits of the wealthy and powerful, and, in the case of *The Devil Tree,* to provide the forces operating on Whalen's youthful development. The distinction from Kosinski's other novels is that the protagonist himself is not, in any important way, autobiographical, as the protagonists in his other works, even in *Steps,* tend to be. It is true that Ivan Sanders, one of the most insightful commentators on Kosinski, has pointed out some surprising parallels between Chance, in *Being There,* and Kosinski. Chance, he points out, because of his isolated beginnings, is an "outsider," a "foreign observer." "Kosinski has often talked about the liberating influence of an adopted language where every word is a new adventure and clichés have real meaning. . . . Chance, like Kosinski, experiences his clichés very profoundly; language to both of them is something external, a contrivance. . . . The image of a rootless, pastless, totally unaffiliated man who sees everything as though for the first time must have fascinated the author."[15]

Nevertheless, Chance is in no important way a projection of Kosinski, or one of the disguises with which he goes forth in the world, as we often feel protagonists of his other novels to be.[16]

Whalen, in *The Devil Tree,* is even less so. Kosinski has remarked, "In my own attitude toward [*The Devil Tree*], I felt a substantial difference throughout the writing of the book; I policed myself not to respond to Whalen, whom I would not like, and not to really comment upon him, since my practicality and my own background would clearly either get rid of certain predicaments of his life or would modify them for him. I had no right to do that. In both *Steps* and *Being There* I was in a position of responding to and commenting upon; they were, so to speak, at my disposal. Here the events and the protagonist were not. I think this is one difference."[17]

Addendum: The Revised Edition of *The Devil Tree*

Kosinski, who revises the final galleys of his novels several times, at great expense to himself and his publishers, is never satisfied with the final form of his works, but continues altering and revising them, so that each new edition of his books contains many changes. He has taken this tendency to its extreme form in the case of *The Devil Tree*.

The new "revised and expanded" edition of *The Devil Tree* has been entirely rewritten. Kosinski tells me he spent seven months at it, and over one third of the material is entirely new. There are no two pages alike between this and the earlier edition, and nearly every sentence has been altered. In an Author's Note at the beginning he says "When I wrote this novel initially, I felt restricted by the proximity of its story to the environment and events of my recent past decade. This might account for the cryptic tone of the novel's first version." The book appeared originally in 1973, so the "recent past decade" would have been the period from 1962 on when he was married to Mary Hayward Weir and lived and traveled in her circles.

The effect of the extensive changes has been (1) to make the novel more regular and straightforward in plot and narration, (2) to make it more autobiographical, and (3) to make it less pessimistic, more hopeful. These are the directions Kosinski's most recent novels have been taking (see chapters 7 and 8), so in effect he has rewritten the novel the way he is now writing, rather than the way he was writing in 1973.

In plot the new version is almost perfectly chronological. At the beginning Whalen has just returned to this country after years of wandering abroad, where he had remained in exile to avoid the draft. During those wanderings he had experimented heavily with drugs, finally requiring extensive treatment to cure him of his addiction to opium. Now he is trying to pick up the pieces of his life again, which involves coming to terms with his relationship with Karen, and deciding what his relationship is going to be with the vast industrial empire he has inherited. By the end of the novel it seems the relationship with Karen is going to come to nothing; though they need each other, they are both too guarded to risk very much with each other. The relationship with his father's industry obviously is at an end, since he has murdered the Howmets, who are his closest link with it. He is left, then, at the end, severed from the past. The severance has been traumatic, but he is beginning to look forward again.

Why do I say the revised edition is more autobiographical? As I explained earlier in this chapter, the original version of the novel used elements out of Kosinski's past as background, but the protagonist, Jonathan Whalen, seemed to be a character very different from Kosinski, a young American from a rich family. His speech patterns, his problems, his concerns, seemed unlike Kosinski's. In the new version, his speech, his concerns, are closer to Kosinski's. The change can be seen most clearly in a number of new episodes, in which Whalen quotes long strings of statistics on how many hours a day the average American watches television, and the effects of this on his development, or on the number of stress-related problems the American businessman suffers from, the high percentage who have admitted they must compromise their own ethical principles in order to continue in their jobs, and so on. The intention is to make clear the troubled society out of which Whalen is attempting to form his own consciousness. But the comments, the statistics, we have heard before from professional sociologist Kosinski, in talks he has given and essays he has written. The effect is to bring Whalen closer to Kosinski himself, and once we begin to make Whalen a disguise for Kosinski, we begin to see many other connections between them.

For example, Whalen has been abroad for several years. Who knows how extreme or cruel or perverse his experiences were? He gives Karen all his diaries from that period, then worries that she will reject him when she sees what things he has done. Kosinski tells us he wrote *The Painted Bird* in part to try to make his past accessible to his wife, whose own experience was so diametrically opposite to his. Kosinski, like so many of his characters, is a "survivor." Can anyone whose own life has been protected and favored ever understand what a "survivor" has had to go through, has had to witness and experience, and perform, in order to survive? And once the survivor has told his story, can the protected and favored person ever again accept him, knowing what he has been capable of?

During the time of his marriage, he had lived the life of the super-rich. He was supported in a lifestyle of opulence and privilege, but he must have asked himself how he should continue in it. Merely as an appendage, a parasite? Who was he himself, and where was his individual destiny? He had of course his novels that he was writing, and so he was able to define himself apart from the world he was swept up in. But when his wife died, his personal connection with that world was gone, and he was freer to examine the sources of that wealth, and find them admirable in a way—his admiration for steel magnate Ernest Weir is great—but also find them immoral. If the first industrial barons who shouldered their way to the top had something redeeming about them just in their size and energy, the hangers-on after them had not. Kosinski's position, he must certainly have seen, was ambiguous, and he severed himself from that part of his life, denying it absolutely, one feels, just as Whalen finally does, taking with him what he has gained in the way of experience and insight, but then making his own way.

And so the final scene of the novel—Whalen, coming out of his break-down, standing on the shore of the lake and looking across at the lights of Geneva—has a different cast to it. One feels that the past is through for him. He is exactly in the present moment, and there is at least the chance that he can now become his own man. It was to clinics in Geneva that Kosinski took his wife in the last days of her illness, so perhaps it was while looking at the blinking lights of Geneva that Kosinski himself first began working out the possibilities of his life now that "recent past decade" had ended for him, now that all that was good and all that was bad in the past had gone, and he was free to make his own way.

Chapter Six
Cockpit

Kosinski has often said that all of his novels are part of a cycle exploring the relationships between the individual and society.[1] No doubt this is true, but the reader most readily perceives the three most recent novels (*Cockpit,* 1975; *Blind Date,* 1977; and *Passion Play,* 1979) as constituting a cycle. At any rate they show a close superficial resemblance to one another in protagonist, structure, tone, and themes and at the same time there is a movement or development from one novel to the next. In the three chapters discussing these novels, among other things I will be interested in charting the progression in these features from one novel to the next.

Cockpit

As with most Kosinski novels, *Cockpit* is difficult to summarize, since there is nothing in the novel that can really be called a plot. Instead, there is a somewhat protean narrator who moves from place to place, experiencing—often creating—various adventures which seem to be tonally or thematically related, and which, by slow accumulation, become at last the experience of the novel.

A difference from earlier novels is that the incidents, or episodes, are markedly longer, and fewer, nineteen different "chapters" in a fairly long novel, as compared to 137 in *The Devil Tree.*

The narrator, Tarden, was formerly a secret agent in the "Service" but has now abandoned it, and since all agents who defect from the Service are hunted down and killed, he is forced to live a mobile, anonymous, disguised life, moving from apartment to apartment, constantly on guard. Unable to live a normal life, he has fleeting, generally unsuccessful relationships with women, and, increasingly, enters secretly into the lives of others, as a kind of self-appointed helper of the needy and punisher of evil. His pleasure, obviously, is in having control over other's lives, and his methods for gaining control—even in a "good" cause—are unscrupulous.

From time to time the novel flashes back to his youth in Eastern Europe, or to his time as a young immigrant just entering the United States, to various jobs in this country and abroad he had in order to eke out a living, until a beautiful Lebanese woman who becomes his lover introduces him to the Service. In all the earlier incidents, before he is in the Service, we see he already had a strong penchant for disguise, and for manipulating the lives of others.

The novel then goes back and forth between episodes in which we see Tarden as an agent, sometimes hunting down other defecting agents, such as he will become; and episodes of Tarden's secretive life after he defected. Towards the end—he is growing older—he finds a rich businessman who has just lost his girl friend and fixes him up with a strikingly attractive girl with a shady past. But he had first made a deal with the girl that, in return for fixing her up with a wealthy man who will advance her career, she must be on constant call for whatever sexual demands Tarden wishes to make on her. She agrees, but once she is fixed up and doing very well, becoming wealthy and famous, she begins ignoring Tarden's demands. Like most Kosinski characters, Tarden has a strong ethic of revenge and makes her the victim of his final terrible scheme. Tarden invites the girl to an air show, and while she is standing in front of a military plane, Tarden (he had earlier bribed the pilot) turns on the plane's radar equipment for a moment, giving the girl— unknown to her—a fatal dose of radiation poisoning.

In the last major incident of the novel, Tarden is trapped for eight hours in an elevator which is constantly going up and down, and he panics paranoiacally.

Tarden's Life before He Entered the Service

Although Tarden (Tarden is only one of his names) sometimes blames his defection from the Service for the reason he must lead such an anonymous, secretive life and have such oblique and fleeting affairs with others, we see in fact his character as a loner, and as a detached manipulator of others, is well marked from childhood. As he says himself, "since I was a child I have done many inexplicable things.

Perhaps the explanations for my behavior, if there are any, are rooted in an area of my past to which I have no access" (110).[2] He gives us some early accounts. When he is four and his Swiss nanny is hugging him in her lap, he takes out a scissors stolen from her sewing basket and stabs her in the breast, causing a great flow of blood. A few months later, he drops a heavy pot out a window, narrowly missing a five-year-old boy, but lacerating his eye with a broken shard. But these are nothing compared to what he does when he is twelve. While his parents are away during the day (it is shortly after the war, in a tightly controlled Eastern European country), he phones numbers at random, and, when he gets an answer, brilliantly mimics the tone of a government administrator, ordering the people to make a long, expensive trip into the Capital in order to get a permit from such-and-such a government office which would allow them to remain in their present lodgings. When dozens of people have been inconvenienced in this way, the police arrive one day and arrest him and his parents. He confesses to having done it by himself, but they hold his father and tutor, assuming they must have put him up to it. Brazenly, he tells one of his interrogators he had better either release him or kill him outright, otherwise he would one day punish the man's wife and children terribly: "I reminded him how adept I was at affecting the lives of people I did not even know." The policeman is sufficiently impressed that after a bit of blustering, he sees to it they are all released. His father "held me at arm's length and said that he did not want to know what reason I had to hurt so many families. My mother hugged me and told me that even though my tutor had been released from prison, he refused to teach me anymore" (118–19).

When he is in high school, "I discovered that, by squeezing my member, I could force it back into my body" (128), giving him the look of an amputee. Holding his member in place with a clamp, he would begin making love to a new girl, but at the critical moment of disrobing, he would confess to his war wound. After momentary shock, the girl, not needing to fear pregnancy, or his aggression, would let herself go with him as she had never been able to do with another. Suddenly, before she knew what he was doing, he would release the clamp. After her initial anger, she would have to admit that he had released new levels of sensuality in her.

At eighteen, he is skiing at a resort. He is a mediocre skier compared to the ski instructors there, but when no one is around he practices over and over again a specialized ski jump in which he ends up on a balcony, having cleared a long stairway. He performs his stunt several times in public and gains some local acclaim. The local ski instructors are angry, knowing it is only a stunt, and he could not compete with them otherwise. But when he challenges them to a competition in his special stunt, they cannot back out. Hoping to impress a pretty girl staying at the resort, he makes her judge of the competition. He makes his own jump successfully, but the first two of the instructors to try it are badly injured. The competition is called off, and he is declared the winner. "When I asked if the girl would walk back to the town with me, she looked at me coldly and refused" (178).

His qualities of ingenuity, mimicry, lonely single-mindedness, perseverance, nerve, and independence demonstrate their survival value when he is a young man, perhaps in his early twenties. He is at war with the totalitarian state, and seeks everywhere for ways to escape. His father had often told him the country was "an endless, bureaucratic jungle," and "I decided to turn that confusion back on itself, to make it work for me" (19). Using his status as a researcher at an important scientific institute, he gets hold of official stationery, and painstakingly invents four patrons who begin writing letters recommending him for study abroad. Ultimately, capitalizing several times on bureaucratic lethargy and inefficiency, playing one functionary off against another—but, just in case, always carrying a cyanide capsule in his pocket—he at last gets his passport and ticket to the United States, where he plans to defect.[3]

Tarden's Life in the Service

In fact we see very little of Tarden's life as an agent. We are told nothing about the Service or its aims. In one brief episode, we see Tarden eliminate a defected agent; in another, he is sent to Indonesia on assignment, but the assignment is aborted; in another, he trains a dog to be a living bomb to help him assassinate someone. After that, when we see him, he has defected, and is the only agent he knows of who still has not been found and eliminated.

Obviously, then, within the economy of the novel, the Service has no real function except to give some rationale for the secretive and marginal life of the protagonist. Perhaps this is what he means by the curious comment he makes about Theodora, the Lebanese woman who had originally introduced him to the Service: "She had helped me find a shield for the self I wanted to hide" (64).

Tarden's Life after the Service

The notion is established at the beginning of the novel that he is a defected agent and, therefore, must live a highly mobile life, trusting no one, confiding in no one, moving from apartment to apartment every few weeks, each apartment arranged and fitted with elaborate escape mechanisms. But once that notion is established, not a great deal of mention is made of the situation, except to remind us of it from time to time. If he is actually being hunted by the Service, we only see brief hints of it once or twice. Any pursuit is not a felt part of the novel.

The novel begins with an open letter by Tarden, perhaps in writing, but most likely only in his head, to a woman he has known a long time, but not intimately. It seems to be a woman he would in the normal course establish perhaps a genuine relationship with. But there can be no normal course for him. "I wanted to invite you to the apartment I rent as Tarden, the only name you know me by," he tells her. But I was afraid that, if I did see you alone, you might be upset by what I had to say, by my desire to share my life with you. I did not want to just tell you about my past. I wanted you to relive it" (2).

Rather than taking her to his apartment, he instead picks up a prostitute, someone with whom he would not be compelled to share more than a moment's physical connection. He has one of his frequent brief seizures while she is there, and it is brought home to him how anonymous and sordid his death would be, should he die in that moment.

The business about his being an agent, now defected, is indeed a shield, a cover, a disguise, but what it disguises is our essential aloneness, our essential transience in time, our constantly present mortality. Kosinski has several times said words to the effect that we are the protagonist of our own life's drama, and when we die the play ends. There is no way we can share this fundamental experience.

Disguise

As an agent, Tarden was frequently obligated to adopt a disguise to cover his activity for the Service. At one time we see him going to Indonesia as part of an international delegation of psychiatrists and anthropologists. At another time he is in Europe as an industrial representative. In neither of these cases does the ensuing episode have anything to do with his work as an agent. In each case, rather, something develops out of the particular role he is playing. We are reminded of the various roles of the multi-personaed protagonists of other Kosinski novels (archaeologist and business representative are favorite roles), and realize that once more Tarden's work as an agent is, in terms of Kosinski's artistic intention, a disguise itself—a cover for the fact of our multiple and shifting selves—another reason it is so difficult for anyone to know us, or for us to know another.

For Tarden, the most instructive example of the essential disguise, or unknowableness, of others, is the case of Robert, his roommate when he first comes to America. Robert is the closest, most considerate, most caring friend he has ever had, the single person he has ever been able to trust fully. Living with him day after day has amply demonstrated Robert's gentle, even, predictable temperament. Then one day Robert chases Tarden around the house for over an hour trying to cut off his head with a carving knife. The police save Tarden at the last second, and Tarden only then learns of Robert's lifelong history of violent mental derangement. He reflects on the experience, "Even now, whenever I become involved with others enough to expect certain patterns of behavior or to rely on them, the memory of my experience with Robert returns to alert me" (48–49).

As for Tarden himself, "I've come to look upon disguise as more than a means of personal liberation: it's a necessity. My life depends on my being able to instantly create a new persona and slip out of the past" (129–30). We are reminded of Kosinski's comments in *The Art of the Self* that the self must constantly get clear from its past in order to live fully in the present moment. We are, of course, a new person in each moment of our lives, a combination of the person created by that moment, and the person we create to meet that moment.

Control of the Self

The key to Tarden's jealously guarded independence is his absolute control of himself. But by "himself" I mean the self he is at any particular moment. There are no "real" selves, only disguises. The disguise, indeed, is the real Tarden.

Once again in the novel, the disguise is a metaphor for his control over himself, so absolute that at each moment he literally creates himself.

In the opening chapter we see all sides of his control. He tells us of the apartments he keeps in every major city, paid for three years in advance, three-digit combination locks on every door, multiple exits, hiding places, electronic controls to set off small explosives in any room he chooses, papers kept in vaults in various locations, he himself moving every few weeks so no one in a particular place sees him often enough to remember him.

With all his safeguards he succeeds in preserving his existence, but we see how great the cost is. First of all, his instinct is to probe deeply into the existence of all those around him. He must know the inmost heart of all those he comes in contact with, just in case they offer a threat to him. But in practical terms that means he cannot have a close human relationship. As with the case of Valerie, in the first chapter, with whom he might have had a quite satisfactory relationship, he could not resist testing her at every opportunity, until finally, almost inevitably, he found some corner of her that was not entirely honest with him. He challenged her, and she simply left him.

Or again, he observes, in the incident of the brief attack he suffers while the prostitute is in his apartment, "I heard the girl singing in my bathroom, and wondered what would happen if I should die right then. It wasn't the thought of dying that disturbed me, but that I might die without leaving a trace" (3). He has devoted himself so thoroughly to anonymity, that, he realizes, the only result can be, at last, anonymous death.

And finally, there is after all a limitation on his control. His body itself asserts a certain autonomy. There are his seizures, when it becomes difficult for him to breathe, when his heartbeat grows irregular, and which could kill him at any moment. He has no way to gaining control over them.

There is his memory: he is blessed—or cursed—with total recall: "If I evoke a single memory picture, others will spring up automatically to join it and soon the montage of a past self will emerge. It's an autonomous process" (13). There is the possibility, then, of that past self overwhelming the self of the present. He was warned as a child, when his remarkable memory was first discovered through school tests, "to memorize only useful information. Otherwise, my mind would become an overcrowded attic, steadily but unselectively storing up everything I saw. One day, they added, the attic might collapse, wrecking the house beneath" (90–91).

Also autonomous is his body's system of healing wounds: "Although I often tried to keep a wound open and bleeding, it always healed itself overnight, challenging my power over myself. I hated the sense of an autonomous force in my body, determining what would happen to me" (13).

Almost worst of all is his irreducible dependence on other human beings. Once when he was at the dentist's, he had a freak reaction to the anesthetic: "I had survived after my heart stopped only because the incident had happened in a clinic. . . . Like the elusive substance that had once healed my wound, now the State had saved me without my consent" (14–15).

If his life cannot always be in his control, at least his death can, giving an added meaning—in the episode where he is trying to escape from Eastern Europe—when he says "I sensed freedom only when my fingers stroked the foil-wrapped [cyanide] pellet in my pocket" (16).

Control of Others

If he began by controlling himself as much as possible, and then his apartment—the immediate environment—working outward by steady concentric circles, he next needed to control the outer environment, which is to say, controlling all the human beings with whom he came in contact.

It is a standard Kosinski theme—the most direct and safest way to preserve oneself as subject is to convert all around one into objects. Tarden devotes himself to interfering in other's lives. It is not always to harm them. Sometimes he is beneficial to them, though usually in rather paltry ways. But even when he works for their benefit, it is an example of his exploiting or using them for his own satisfaction.

He explains that when he was a boy he had an old bicycle wheel he used to roll before him, guiding it with a stick, making it do whatever he wanted. He was not satisfied unless he was driving it somewhere, making it obedient to all his demands. Now, because of defecting from the Service, he is forced to lead his lonely anonymous life. "Yet, to live alone," he repines, "depending on no one, and to keep up no lasting associations, is like living in a cell; and I have never lost my desire to be as free as I was as a child, almost flying, drawn on by my wheel. Now, I have devised a new kind of wheel game, which provides the human associations my current lifestyle prohibits. Confronted with hundreds of anonymous faces, hundreds of human wheels, I choose one. . . . I pick a life and enter it, unobserved" (148).

Even in his very best actions, there is a kind of patronizing meanness. For instance, he likes to find an older, tired-looking saleslady and give her a very bad time, making her bring out dozens of models from the storeroom of whatever he pretends to want to buy, then saying he has changed his mind. If she is unfailingly courteous (if Tarden were in the saleslady's place, and someone treated him like that, he would plot a diabolical revenge) then she earns her reward—a letter to the president of the company saying how courteous she was.

Usually, however, his preferred way of being a benefactor is not to help the needy, but rather to punish the wrongdoer. That way he is able to do good by harming someone.

I am describing here my own response as reader to Tarden's actions. But evidently Kosinski does not intend to have him judged quite so harshly, as his words to Gail Sheehy suggest: "My protagonists do not isolate themselves. They are adventurers but also self-appointed reformers of an unjust world: they interfere on behalf of the weak and the fallen and the disfigured. I see this as an important part of the philosophy of the self: you cannot be faithful to your own sense of drama if you disregard the drama in the life of others—those right next to you."[4]

The Scourge of God

The notion of his protagonists as "self-appointed reformers of an unjust world" is an old notion, the notion of the "scourge of God," of someone placed on earth for the purpose of enacting God's justice. It is first mentioned in Kosinski's work—ironically, to be sure—when the superstitious peasants in *The Painted Bird* feel that the Nazis are God's instrument of revenge against the Jews who killed Christ (84). We next notice the scene in *Steps* where the protagonist causes some soldiers to be blown up, because a soldier had shot down two civilians apparently just for the pleasure of it (31–32).

In *Cockpit* the idea of the protagonist as scourge of God is first fully worked out, reaching its final development in Kosinski's next novel, *Blind Date*. We see Tarden robbing mail sacks to get letters to read as an entrée into others' lives. In one letter he reads that the father of the family, who had escaped from an Eastern European country twenty-five years before, was arrested and imprisoned in that country when the airplane he was traveling on made an unscheduled stop there. Tarden carefully investigates the UN ambassador from that country, finds out he had been involved in a real-estate kickback deal to rob his country of a great deal of money. Tarden threatens the man with exposure if he does not use his weight to have the other man released and returned to America. On another occasion, when he learns through his snooping that a best-selling author who was creating a stir because he had been arrested in East Germany has actually trumped up the whole story just to boost sagging book sales, he intervenes, and the man is found dead in his car, killed by carbon monoxide fumes.

In its origins, the scourge of God motif is an offshoot of two qualities in Kosinski's protagonists. One, the wish for control over others. When Tarden finds, in one of his stolen letters, a situation that it looks like he might intervene in, "I feel I have found a magic passport to another's life, as well as control over it" (155). Two, it is obviously an offshoot of the revenge theme that we have examined in Kosinski's other novels.

The Revenge Theme

Though Kosinski, as we have seen, speaks for the new social consciousness of his protagonists as "self-appointed reformers," in fact most of the elaborate revenges Tarden carries out are absolutely personal actions directed against people who have crossed him, and the only heinous "crime" most of these people have committed has been to resist being controlled by him.

Revenge begins on a small scale in the novel, but steadily accelerates.[5] When we first see Tarden in action, he catches his girl friend with a lover, sneaks up on them while they are sleeping, and takes a number of pictures of them. When, later, he confronts the girl with the pictures, she has no idea how he could have taken them. He hints to her that he and her lover had arranged it together, for the sake of getting the photos. She storms out, furious with both men.

While Tarden is engineering his escape from Eastern Europe, he has some of his imaginary sponsors request letters of recommendation from Tarden's actual teachers—the letters of course all coming to Tarden, so that he could remove negative ones. One of his professors, who had written a very negative letter, years later is himself trying to get entry into America. He comes to Tarden for help in being allowed to stay in America, saying that, after all, he had helped Tarden in the past. Tarden is able to produce the letter the man had written, and the man leaves, crestfallen.

When Tarden is in Indonesia at a convention of psychiatrists and anthropologists, he makes fun of a newlywed husband who is attending the conference. The man's wife becomes quite hostile with Tarden because of his joking. For this crime he sneaks into her dormitory and, threatening that he will kill her husband with a special poison ring he had demonstrated to her earlier, forces her into demeaning sexual acts with him.

He begins spending time photographing a prostitute. When her tough pimp knocks Tarden down one night, because the photography was taking up so much of the girl's working time, Tarden plants a substance in the pimp's car that looks like heroin, and the pimp is killed by the police.[6]

So far they have been standard revenges such as we are accustomed to find in Kosinski novels. Throughout the novel, Kosinski has somehow kept us in the main sympathetic with his protagonist, though his actions are often distasteful. But Tarden's final, most elaborate revenge goes some way toward turning the reader against him.

Tarden tells a beautiful girl that he will fix her up with a millionaire businessman on condition that she will always be on call for Tarden for whatever he wants. She agrees and is soon married to the man. She gets a press agent and begins building her career (despite boredom with her husband), working on a novel, and coming to Tarden less and less often when he calls. So he gets her to his apartment, binds her hand and foot, gets three derelicts ("two blacks and a white" [222]) out of a gutter and has them gang rape her and defecate on her. She takes a shower and shrugs it off, untouched by the experience. Tarden discovers she has a boyfriend, searches his apartment, and finds letters suggesting she plans to murder her husband, who is leaving her everything. Tarden goes to her to blackmail her, and she laughs him away. So he has one last date with her, at an air show, and while she stands in front of a jet plane, he turns on its radar (having bribed the pilot previously) briefly, enough to give her fatal radiation poisoning.

The reader by this time is completely on the side of the brazen girl. She has just the qualities—nerve, persistence, single-mindedness, control—that one would expect Tarden to admire, since they are his own qualities. But evidently there is no room for admiration in Tarden's desperate struggle for dominance.

Tarden's Relations with Women

I say "desperate" in the preceding sentence because in all the relationships he attempts to establish with other human beings, almost invariably with women, Tarden is a failure. Perhaps it is because in each relationship he insists on absolute control, and he does not claim his control by the power of his person, but rather uses either money or some other sort of lever, blackmail, or some sort of contractual arrangement that forces compliance with his will. He becomes, to the others, that totalitarian State which he could not endure to have over himself, and the women cannot endure it either.

At the beginning of the novel, he tells Valerie that he will set up an unconditional trust fund for her, forever liberating her from work, if she will quit her job and come live with him. "I assured her that I did not expect her to love me. She would live with me, but she would be as free as I to see other people."

Valerie sees through his offer, and tells him that "by appointing myself her liberator, I was actually prohibiting her from shaping her own existence; I was concerned only with my own future and had created an illusion of what I wanted her to be" (6). As I described above, he sets an elaborate trap to catch her and photograph her with her boyfriend. But the upshot is, she simply leaves him.

We have observed him forcing his sex on the psychiatrist's wife or getting the girl in the ski lodge to judge his ski-jumping contest with the other ski instructors, but in each case they display only contempt for him. We see him in other humiliating affairs. In another episode he meets the tall, exquisite wife of an important political leader. He instantly propositions her, and she later comes to a hotel to meet him. He worries and worries that he will not be good enough to please her, and in the end is completely impotent. "God spare beautiful women from men with imagination," she says, before departing (85). In another episode he tries to get a girl, who is part of a father-daughter carnival act, to leave with him. She is incensed: she is all her father has, and his dependency on her gives her life meaning. Their act is to have the father throw heavy extra-size iron horseshoes at her neck; they always land harmlessly on her protective shoulder pads. When Tarden persists in his attentions to her, though she is clearly contemptuous of him, she finally challenges him to stand and be a target for her father, who at the time is nearly passing out with drunkenness. If he survives, he can have his will of the girl.

He accepts the challenge, and the horseshoe lands harmlessly on his shoulder guard. But when he takes the girl to a motel to claim his winnings, he finds her physically impenetrable. "'It would take surgery to open me up,' she said. 'I've never wanted to have the operation.' 'Why not?' 'Because of men like you'" (147).

In both this abortive relationship, and the one with the woman with whom he was impotent, the contest was not for sex but for control. Perhaps Tarden was instinctively impotent with the woman because he felt that, rather than seducing her, he was in fact being used by her. A fatherly doctor he had gone to for potency pills had advised him that he was turning himself "into an instrument to satisfy an aging, adulterous wife." "I am nobody's instrument," he had claimed (78), but maybe the doctor's description of his position struck home. With the carnival girl, he had insisted to her that her father was using her, and she should come with him. She readily sees that he means to use her himself, and actually, with her father, she dominates, she runs things, she makes the act possible. Far from being used, she uses her father to define herself.

Tarden's most complex struggle, however, is with the Lebanese woman who first introduced him to the Service, Theodora. He first meets her in Europe, where she is the wife of a wealthy industrialist. She asks him to give her English lessons, and in a short time they become lovers. But "our physical intimacy only increased the ambiguity of our relationship. She said that she wanted to be more than an afterthought tacked onto the main part of my existence. She wanted to be the center of my life and would not settle for less. Since she knew this need made unreasonable demands upon me, to spare me, she suggested we . . . part" (52).

Nonetheless, they keep coming back together. Tarden is a bit puzzled to discover that, despite her intensity with him, she seems to have another lover as well. She is moving to America and wants Tarden to come back there with her. He claims he cannot afford the trip. She gets a secret document from her other lover and gives it to Tarden. He is able to sell it to the American government for a large sum of money, and the transaction is also his entrée into the Service.

He then finds out she also had been an operative in the Service, but had been dropped for failing a mission. Her marriage to the indus-trialist had just been a cover; so it was terminated. When Tarden sees her again, she is aged and obese. She has lost several jobs, and is barely making a living. Though she is getting old, and knows it may be too late, she has decided to have a baby.

Tarden is not interested in servicing her, but when she promises to supply him daily with his choice of any kind of girl he wants, the only stipulation being that she can collect his semen at the end, he cannot resist. The operation seems to work better if Theodora herself arouses the girls, and remains to witness the act.

She tells everyone she is pregnant and then that she has had a son. No one believes her. When Tarden tries to see it, she says that, learning she had bone cancer and would not be able to care for it, she had given it to foster parents to raise. He is convinced she is lying. When Tarden next sees her, she is in the last days of her terminal illness. He notices a Polaroid picture of a child in a playpen. She does not speak to him and is dead a few days later.

Tarden then learns from a nurse that she had indeed had a son. Each day, while she waited in the hospital to die, she had made herself up, put on a wig, and dressed attractively, waiting for Tarden to come to her. He had not, so finally she had lost interest and let herself go. It was only then that Tarden had come, and she had not spoken to him.

Tarden tries to trace the child, but no one will tell him who the foster parents are. It is explained to him that the son will never be told he is adopted.

We recall that Theodora had said that she did not want to be "an afterthought tacked onto the main part of my existence. She wanted to be the center." She has in a sense succeeded, for she now has taken control of his future.

He has in fact fallen into the trap he set for Valerie, who had had the prescience to see that "I was actually prohibiting her from shaping her own existence; I was concerned only with my own future."

He was still a young man when Theodora used him to produce a son for the sake of her own future. By the time he makes his contractual arrangement with the girl at the end of the novel, the girl who conveniently forgets her obligations to him, he is "a bony old bird," as he calls himself frequently. The young girl, with her brash nerve, her ambition to achieve what she wants by any means, her single-minded perseverance, is like his own youth, as he himself moves steadily to old age and death. He had given her her start, and once more, as with Theodora, he finds she has used him for the sake of her own future. Is this why he is so unforgiving? The blast from the radar equipment will kill the girl with the cancer Theodora died from. Is it the typical gambit of a Kosinski protagonist of getting revenge on somebody, even if not precisely the one who has injured you? Is it Theodora he is paying back?

The Present Moment

But destroying the girl in a sense is destroying his own past, as Theodora has destroyed his ability to have his own future. He is left squarely in the present moment, the lone aging survivor, nothing ahead but anonymous death.

"Whenever I am in a large city, I often go for walks around three or four o'clock in the morning. I feel like a solitary visitor in a vast, private museum. At that hour, one can easily imagine that mankind is nearly extinct . . . that I am one of the few survivors left to contemplate the urban remains" (236).

It is worth pointing out that the events of the novel are not always to be taken strictly literally. *Cockpit* is as well a symbolical, a philosophical novel. Tarden's lonely walk through the early morning streets presents a paradox. His position as a lonely wanderer, an aging survivor with only bleak anonymous death for future, is in fact the essential condition of man on this planet. We blind ourselves to our condition, living in the past, in the future, trusting in our hospitals, our armies to protect us, convincing ourselves that loneliness and pain and death happen only to someone else. Tarden, bereft of past and future, sees clearly and coldly the actual present. If it is illusionless, at least it is the truth. And indeed there is a sort of lonely splendor in his "vast, private museum." He is in truth "one of the few survivors," for those who do not have a true picture of their existence in the present moment are not truly living, have withdrawn from life in hopes of escaping the inevitable pains of life.

The point is neatly made as the episode continues: during one of his early morning walks, Tarden comes to a part of the city he particularly likes, finds an apartment that exactly suits his needs, and tries to rent it. He finds out, however, that it is already rented by an aging bachelor who only leaves the apartment twice a week. The superintendent warns him that he will never get the old man to move. But he does not know Tarden.

Tarden deluges the man with mail, brightly colored ads of retirement communities in Florida, clippings showing the escalating rates of crime against the elderly in cities, the sky-rocketing costs of urban living, the health effects of pollution.

The superintendent phones Tarden: the old bachelor has moved to Florida. The man has given up the pain and risks of life in the city—the city representing life in the present moment. What has he gained? Tarden visits the old-age community in Florida. It is one of the most horrific scenes in the novel. The residents are all senile and talk constantly about outliving each other and play chicken at the table, seeing who can stay there the longest without having to go to the bathroom. Sitting in the midst of them is "it," a thing continuing its ravaged life beyond all reason.

The Elevator and the Skating Rink

The novel ends with two brief, obviously symbolical scenes. In the first, Tarden, leaving his apartment one night, is trapped in the elevator for eight hours, the elevator constantly going to the top, then straight back down to the bottom, then bouncing back up to the top, never pausing, the doors never opening. The temperature rises, Tarden becomes weakened by the water loss from his profuse sweating. He strips himself naked, he vomits, he defecates, he shouts and bangs at the doors, but there is no one to hear, till the following morning. He is in "a windowless cell. The forces that propelled it up and down seemed as arbitrary and autonomous as those that spin the earth on its axis. Here, in the solitude of my capsule, I sensed a curious time warp. . . . I was completely cut off from my past; a royal mummy, safely cradled and sealed for the long voyage ahead" (247).[7]

It is another image of the bare truth of our existence in the present moment. Interestingly, what is stressed here—in a novel in which control has been so important—is how little actual control we have. All we really have, for the preserving of our human dignity, is the control over ourselves, our insisting that we continue to live in the present with full awareness of our true position.

In the next scene, he looks down from his window at night onto a lighted skating rink. "The skaters move smoothly in their circle of light, gliding in uninterrupted movement to slow, silent music. From the rink's apron other figures spill onto the ice, find an opening and blend in with the flow." It is the image of the collective, the skaters blending safely together, giving up their individuality to the rhythm of the music imposed on them from outside. An odd optical illusion stresses their abnegation of life, their nonliving stance: "Now the rink appears to revolve around the skaters as they stand like frozen sculptures growing out of the ice."[8]

Cutting across the image of the frozen skaters comes Tarden's memory of "a great old army tank, hit decades ago by an enemy shell, sunken in a shallow lagoon. . . . Its corroded gun defiantly trains on trenches and machine-gun nests, long buried in the sands of a deserted beach" (last three quotes, 248).

It is the final image of the book, a lone dead battler in a lost and forgotten war. It is meaningless, except for the qualities of dignity and defiance. But in a world where we must choose between the loneliness of the endless elevator ride or blend into the frozen living death of the circling skaters, dignity and defiance are all we are left with—a bleak Nordic vision in which the best we can ask is to be allowed to fight honorably against overwhelming odds until the moment of final defeat.

The Meaning of the Title

The "cockpit" is, naturally, the cockpit of the jet plane Tarden crawls into to activate the radar equipment. But Kosinski in interviews, has suggested several meanings for the word. It is the pit in which cocks do battle. It is the special enclosed space for pilots or sailors. "But the cockpit," he observes, "also represents the technological environment which sets us apart from nature. It is also the artificial skating rink which I describe at the end of the novel." Earlier in the interview he had spoken of "the modern world where millions of persons live prisoners in cages of steel, buildings and automobiles." These are negative images, and he claims that in his work "I exhort people to leave the 'cockpit' . . . to recover the dialogue with the trees."[9]

But there is one more sense in which the word is used, which is suggested by the epigraph, an epigraph which might well stand as a brief résumé of the novel itself, of Tarden sporting with the world which eventually will annihilate him. It is by another philosophical loner who chose always to live in the present moment, the famous pilot, Antoine de Saint-Exupéry, who describes himself sitting alone, braced single-handedly against all forces, in the cockpit of his airplane. "But I dwell now well in the making of the future. Little by little, time is kneading me into shape. A child is not frightened at the thought of being patiently turned into an old man. He is a child and he plays like a child. I too play my games. I count the dials, the levers, the buttons, the knobs of my kingdom."

Kosinski has said "I am astonished that so few of those who have written about *Cockpit* . . . realized that Tarden . . . might generate a feeling of optimism, a sudden inner statement in a reader. Look how much Tarden does with his life."[10]

Autobiographical Elements

I have paused in each of my discussions of Kosinski's books so far to discuss the way he has utilized autobiography in writing them. The first two books, nonfiction, ostensibly used his actual autobiography, as they purport to be journals of his studies in Russia, but though he is at the center of the books as recorder or narrator, in the main he quotes the words of others. We did notice, however, the way in which he made himself protagonist of certain episodes, on occasion, which were presented to make some thematic point. For example, when he was discussing the puritanical policies of the State, he told the story of his girl friend who was ostracized and punished when she began dressing in a Western style in order to please him.

The Painted Bird, Kosinski's first novel, used, evidently, events very close to happenings in Kosinski's own childhood to tell its story, though, as I tried to indicate in my discussion of that novel, the events were transmuted to fiction, were made subservient to the novel's artistic aims—just as, indeed, some of the events in the nonfiction books may have been altered or arranged to serve their thematic ends.

In *Steps* we noticed episodes which seemed to be very close to Kosinski's actual experiences when first arriving in the United States and concluded that in a novel which made a point of insisting that we look at each of its incidents in isolation from the others, the autobiographical incidents were included at least partly because they were so intrinsically interesting, made such good stories, in addition to stressing the fullness of life at the present moment.

Being There and *The Devil Tree* made use of events from the period of Kosinski's life when he was married to Mary Weir and was living in incredible luxury. Mainly the scenes were utilized to give convincing background details for the wealthy people in those novels.

With *Cockpit,* Kosinski begins using autobiography in a different way, a way he will continue to develop in the next two novels. First of all, as in previous novels, he utilizes bits of his own biography fairly directly in suitable parts of the novel. We have noted, for example, that the episode in which he escapes from the Eastern European country of his birth and the episode in which he is trapped in the elevator are both directly autobiographical. There are other details. Tarden describes an ingenious hiding place he has in his apartment (4). Evidently Kosinski has one like it in his own apartment (see Chapter 1). We see Tarden walking the streets of the city at three and four in the morning, and Kosinski has often said this is a habit of his.

So far all is standard Kosinski practice, the utilizing of autobiographical material as grist for his stories. What is subtly different in *Cockpit* from previous Kosinski novels is that Tarden, turned into a new person not Kosinski, in a way begins to *stand for* Kosinski, to be a symbol for him, a "disguise" for him, and the story of Tarden begins to be a spiritual autobiography of Kosinski himself, told by indirection.

Tarden, as Kosinski, first defects from the collectivized Eastern European "State." Upon arriving in the United States, Tarden joins a new State, the "Service." But soon he has defected from that as well, as Kosinski, perhaps, left his graduate studies, his training for a workaday life, the second defection, which would leave him, as it left Tarden, a permanent loner on the margins of society, as the full-time artist in this country must always be.

Though I cannot support my speculation in any way, I note with interest that Theodora, perhaps the most important woman in his life—at least in the shaping of his life—is the first to introduce him to the highest, most rarified echelons of the Service (which I have equated with the System), from which he emerges a wealthy man. She is much older than he, initially married to a powerful industrialist and demands a central role in his life, a controlling power in his destiny. Her battle for control of him is the most powerful and subtle that Tarden faces and continues even after she has died of cancer.

What I am coming to is that if in certain ways Tarden is a highly disguised and transfigured version of Kosinski, then Theodora may be in certain ways a highly disguised and transfigured version of Mary Weir, a woman several years older than Kosinski when they married and who introduced him into the highest levels of the American business community, a System or Establishment from which he has since defected to develop himself as an artist. Like Tarden, though he has defected, he has kept many of the values and techniques of that system to aid him in his life as lone antagonist of the System—Kosinski is an excellent businessman, managing all his own book contracts and working very skillfully to advance his career. Mary Weir, of course, died of cancer, but her influence on Kosinski's life—as we readily see in his writing—continues.[11]

Once make Tarden a "disguise" for Kosinski as artist, then we have a new light on the intensity with which he tries to control people, as a self-appointed reformer. For what does Kosinski tell us his constant task as artist is, but to shock, to awaken us into life? What does he attack us for but our cowardice, our refusal to see every moment as precious? We have said that Tarden in his efforts to control the destinies of the other characters is in every important case a failure, because in each he has only strengthened the others in their own insistence on controlling their own destinies. Paradoxically, such failures would be successes for Kosinski. Kosinski as self-appointed reformer of our lives seeks to control us as readers, but the control he wants over us, through shock, through awakening, is to force us to take control of our own lives.[12]

Chapter Seven
Chance, Angst, and Necessity in *Blind Date*

I suggested in the last chapter that with *Cockpit* Kosinski began exploring some new directions. In *Blind Date,* many of the tendencies barely perceived in *Cockpit* have become much more obvious. In particular, the idea of the protagonist being a disguise for Kosinski, and the actions of the novel representing Kosinski's spiritual autobiography are much more clearly evident.

Blind Date

The novel is presented in the by now standard Kosinski fashion: a series of incidents which find the mobile lone-wolf protagonist in various countries, frequently flashing back to the past, moving from adventure to adventure, from woman to woman. Levanter, the protagonist, calls himself a "small investor," an idea man, someone who makes his living by capitalizing on the chance events of the moment.

We first see him vacationing in a Swiss ski lodge. He meets Pauline, a pianist, who had studied with the same teacher his mother had long ago studied with. He says his mother had been the teacher's mistress. Pauline says, if I was also the teacher's mistress, does that mean I am connected with your mother? Levanter says, if I was my mother's lover, does that mean I am connected with you?

In fact, we discover, Levanter had for several years been his mother's lover, and later in the novel his connection with Pauline will indeed be very special.

We next see him making money in some ingenious and typically unscrupulous business deals, or cleverly punishing some people who have insulted him. We also learn that he is growing old and not skiing as well as he used to be able to. Also—a new note—we see him in comic episodes, of which he is often the butt.

Levanter's heart beats to its own rhythm. When it is calm, he is calm. When it is agitated, he must perform some adventurous action. When he discovers the head of internal affairs of some totalitarian country, a man famous for arrests, tortures, and deaths, is skiing incognito at the lodge, he ingeniously manages to blow him up. His heart is calm again, and the incident passes quickly from his memory. His heroes are the Israelis who hunt down the German war criminals one by one.

He meets his old friend Romarkin in Paris, and there is a flashback to the time when they were both students in Eastern Europe, got into serious trouble with the State, and were forced to join the army. Subsequently, they have both managed to escape to the West.

As a child at camp, Levanter had met Oscar, a boy a few years older, who was an accomplished and experienced rapist. In his special code, he calls the girls he rapes "blind dates." He teaches Levanter his techniques, and Levanter one day follows and rapes a young girl with whom he is secretly infatuated. The next year he meets the same girl; they get along well together and are about to become lovers, when he kisses her in the way the rapist had, and she realizes it was he and leaves in a rage.

Levanter meets several people whom we recognize as real, rather than fictional characters: Stalin's daughter Svetlana, Charles Lindbergh, the biologist Jacques Monod (who tells him that blind chance is responsible for each random event in life), and most disturbingly, the people who were in Sharon Tate's house on the night of the Manson murders. The night of the murders is graphically recreated in the novel.

Levanter has an intense affair with the Foxy Lady, a beautiful woman with whom he has every kind of sex except actual intercourse, since she is still bandaged from a recent operation on that part of her body. Then to his shock Levanter discovers she is actually a man who has just had a sex-change operation. Levanter is unable to continue the relationship.

He meets Serena, a mysterious woman who comes to him when she wants to and leaves when she wants to, saying nothing whatever about herself, or where she goes or what she does when she is gone. When she kills a madman in self-defense and Levanter thinks to explain what has happened to the police, she says no, hide the body. She is a well-known

prostitute, and they would never believe her. Levanter is suddenly in a
panic that he may have caught a disease from her. She says all life is
chance, and leaves, never to return again.

Under circumstances very much like those under which Kosinski
met Mary Weir, Levanter meets Mary-Jane Kirkpatrick, an immensely
wealthy heiress; they marry, and she later dies of a brain tumor.

Toward the end of the novel, by complete chance, he rediscovers
Pauline, the pianist of the opening pages, and they come together in a
sexual act which seems to suggest the fulfillment of their relationship,
each giving himself up to the other.

We see Levanter on the ski slopes; the season is over, everyone is
gone. He makes one last descent, equating the descent on skis with life
itself. Fog surges in. He has not dressed sufficiently warmly; he
becomes lost and slowly freezes to death. But he seems to be at peace,
thinking he has always done as well as possible with his life and, at his
age, perhaps deserves a small rest.

The Scourge of God

There were signs that in *Cockpit* Kosinski's protagonist was moving
away from a personal revenge ethic and toward a more impersonal role
as self-appointed reformer of an unjust world, a sort of "scourge of
God." In *Blind Date* the tendency has gone much further. There is little
in the way of personal revenge; but as impersonal "scourge of God"
Levanter is very active, and on an international scale.

We see him in two elaborate actions. In the first, when he overhears
at a party that the minister of internal affairs of some small dictatorship,
notorious for mass arrests, tortures, and murders, will be skiing
incognito at one of Levanter's favorite resorts, Levanter, after extensive
planning, manages to set his skis aboard the gondola the minister and
his two body guards are taking to the top of the ski slope. It is a time of
day when few witnesses are about. As the gondola is swinging over a
thousand-foot-deep chasm, Levanter uses a remote control device to
detonate charges concealed in the skis.

His emotions after the assassination are curious. He is at first elated,
but "by the time he heard the first sketchy radio reports about the
explosion . . . [he] was already feeling it was something he had done
long ago" (38).[1]

Later, Levanter's careful investigations show him that the desk clerk in an American hotel where Eastern European visitors stay is actually an agent of an Eastern European country whose job is to put surveillance equipment in the rooms and eavesdrop for evidence of disloyalty from the visitors. Numerous guests have been arrested upon their return home, thanks to his work. Levanter first begins investigating him when a man he knows, a world-champion saber fencer, is arrested in his home country, has his arm cripplingly broken, and is sentenced to twenty-five years in prison due in part to information given by the desk-clerk informer. Levanter finds a pretext to have a clandestine meeting with the desk clerk in a Turkish bath, overpowers him, ties him to a table in their private stall, puts a saber into the opening of his anus, then rams it to the hilt up into his body.

Again, "scarcely an hour had passed since the clerk had entered Levanter's room at the baths. But what had taken place there had already receded into a remote corner of his memory" (161).

Kosinski stresses the impersonality of the actions, as though Levanter were merely a vehicle through which justice is meted out. The moment before Levanter inserted the saber, he "reminded himself that what he was about to carry out was impersonal revenge, as simple as the verdict of a military tribunal" (160).

Humor

A new and certainly unexpected ingredient in *Blind Date* is humor. There is perhaps a sort of mordant wit in *Being There,* but generally we think of Kosinski's novels as grim and unremitting. Certainly we are not accustomed to scenes designed to elicit a smile from the reader.

It is not, unfortunately, Kosinski's best vein. Humor is generally a question of speed, timing, and surprise. The finest humor is unforced and grows as if naturally out of its situation. And in fiction, humor derives from language as often as from scene. Kosinski's humor tends to be lengthily set up, overly insisted on, and heavy-handed, and to reside solely in situation. The episode in the rented estate in *Cockpit* (see Chapter 6, note 6) in which noisy picnickers are chased off by toy submarines loaded with remote controlled charges and Indian chants follow them about the woods from various concealed loudspeakers, we realize, after the fact, was meant to be hilariously funny. Perhaps in a movie played for slapstick farce it would have worked, but on the printed page it seems wooden and pointless.

In *Blind Date* there are many more scenes attempting humor, and many fail as dismally. In one scene Levanter goes to interview an African diplomat. He is talking to the attractive young white woman who claims to be his secretary when the diplomat himself casually enters the room nearly naked. Obviously the woman is not his secretary, as she was trying to pretend, but his lover. Done quickly in a movie, with perfectly timed cutting on the double takes on the various faces, the scene might have been funny. But Kosinski sits on the scene and insists on it, and Levanter seems to give a knowing smirk to the reader to show he is in on the joke and, of course, much to liberated to be offended, in fact he is actually amused, and so on. Another highly elaborated and lengthily set up scene has to do with Levanter going to visit a small town which—to the town's surprise—is going to host a national convention of midgets. Again in a film there might be a form of humor—not very high—when the townspeople idly note a midget walking by, then stop when they see another, then start when they see another. But in the novel it is not very good. The episode develops more promisingly, and more interestingly, when the midgets are forgotten, and Levanter is trapped in the town in a power play of small-town revenge.

The Protagonist as Butt

One problem in the examples of Kosinski's humor I have given is that in each case the protagonist has been the one on top of the situation. We are to identify with him and laugh at the others, who usually are shown to be inferior to "us" in some way, as the townspeople where the midgets have come to their convention are shown to be obtuse and reactionary.

But there is another development in *Blind Date* which had not been present in the earlier novels, though it was predicted by Tarden's many failures in *Cockpit*. In *Blind Date,* though Levanter is generally on top of situations, as we expect Kosinski protagonists to be, he is very often the butt of the situation, with the humor at his expense. The humor is less insisted on than in other incidents, and, because it is at Levanter's expense, it does not have the slightly nasty patronizing manner of some of the examples I have given.

I am thinking of the scene from Levanter's youth in Eastern Europe when he qualifies as a ski instructor. He is allowed to take long vacations from his university work to live in his favorite ski country working as a ski instructor and giving the other instructors ideology lessons—a small price to pay. The instructors have no education, so need his lectures; but, on the other hand, they have spent their whole lives on skis and are infinitely better skiers than he is. In the cross-country race all the instructors regularly take part in, Levanter, trying his very best, still comes in several hours behind them. He tells them that he will pass them on their tests if they will refrain from beating him by such a sizable margin. In the next race, to everyone's surprise, they all come in in the slowest time since records have been kept.

The New Kosinski Protagonist

This is a new note in Kosinski's novels. It is part of an effort to make the protagonist more human, more vulnerable. As in *Cockpit,* we are told over and over again that the protagonist is aging, that he is less capable of physical actions than he was when he was younger.

His actions have slightly different motivations. We have noted the large, impersonal actions of international justice. On a smaller scale, when he sees some men go the highest most dangerous ski slope with a woman who obviously is a terrified novice skier, he forces them to take off their skis and walk her back to a safe position. When one of the men snaps, "In whose name are you doing this?" he replies, "Simple humanity" (28). In *Cockpit* Tarden performed some generous actions, but in each case his motive seemed to be mainly the pleasure of exerting his will on others. When Levanter says that simple humanity is his motive, we believe him.

In one of the few personal-revenge actions in the novel, Levanter's behavior is instructive. He is wearing his most modish ski attire and carrying the finest equipment that can be bought, when he hears three Russian tourists making fun of him. To their amazement, he suddenly challenges them in fluent Russian, saying he is a lieutenant colonel in

the Soviet Ski Team and he is going to report them for disparaging
Russian athletes. He demands to see their passports, and takes down all
their names.

So far, it is a standard Kosinski scene. But a few minutes later, when
he sees them in nervous conference, no doubt preparing for the investigation that would await them at home, "for a moment he felt sorry for
them and considered going over to apologize and tell them the truth
. . . then he felt ashamed and somehow unnerved by his deception."
For one thing, "to his surprise, the short encounter with the Soviets had
resurrected a part of himself he had believed to be buried, the enjoy-
ment of having certifiable power. When he had terrified those three
Russian mice, he had actually felt himself being transformed into a
Soviet lieutenant colonel" (21).

The touches of humor at Levanter's expense, his refraining from all
but mild personal revenges and then being sorry about those, and his
feeling of uneasiness that a part of him seems to enjoy having power
over others—these are certainly new developments in Kosinski's writing, and the point is that they are programmatic, were first sketched
out with Tarden in *Cockpit,* are carried considerably further with
Levanter, and will be carried further still with Fabian, the protagonist
of Kosinski's next novel, *Passion Play.*

Control

In previous Kosinski novels, characters worked to have complete
control over themselves and others and tried to avoid being controlled
by others and by the State. In *Blind Date* as well control is an issue, but
with important differences.

To begin with, Levanter is notably less successful at maintaining
"control" than previous protagonists have been. When a girl he wants
to see calls unexpectedly, he must call friends and break a prior
engagement: "He would apologize: here he was an investor, he joked,
who wanted to be master of his fate yet couldn't even master his leisure
time" (185). When he achieves his ambition of going out with a
glamorous Russian woman he had always dreamed of, he is powerless to
make love to her; the Russian language they speak works as a resistless
chaperone: how could he make a lewd suggestion to her in the language
of Pushkin? When he picks up a girl in a small town and has a brief

affair with her, he is forced against his will to remain in the town to testify against her in her divorce trial. Even his heart does not beat to the rhythm he asks of it: "Until a few years earlier, he had believed that his heart merely responded to his mind, that it acted in uncomplicated, clockwork response to the sovereign brain. But at times like this he knew the heart dictated sensation and that if the crude, simple pump falters, Levanter could not make it work properly; his brain could do nothing more than react with intense terror." So he stops fighting it. "When his heart was restless, he crowded his schedule with events and people. When his heart was calm, Levanter enjoyed living day by day, unconcerned about either chance or necessity." (30).

Chance and Necessity

There is an epigraph to *Blind Date* by Jacques Monod, the Nobel Prize–winning biologist. The epigraph is from his book, *Chance and Necessity,* a book which has had a strong influence on Kosinski. The book attempts to prove scientifically that though living forms are obviously purposive in their actions, there is still no necessary, predictable direction for life to take, no preordained destiny. Rather, everything is based on the chance juxtapositions of the moment, the result of totally unrelated chains of actions intersecting by blind coincidence.

"Chance" had occasionally been a factor in past Kosinski novels (it was, after all, the name of the protagonist of *Being There*), but only began to emerge as a strong thematic statement in *Cockpit.* In that novel there are two successive scenes which turn on sheer coincidence. In the first we see Tarden, as secret agent, assigned to hunt down and eliminate another agent who had defected. After a long search, no trace of the agent has been found, and Tarden has given up. Then driving by chance through a town, he spots a sports car of just the model the agent used to favor. He cannot overtake the car, but later, hanging around in the town now, he spots, he believes, the agent crossing the street. Outside a camera shop, he studies pictures taken by local photographers, finds the agent's picture, traces him through it, and kills him. It is only then he again sees the sports car and discovers it does not belong to the agent, but is being driven by someone else; then he sees the man he had taken to be the agent crossing the street, and with a closer look realizes he has only a casual resemblance to the agent. Those two complete coincidences had made him stop in the town where the agent actually is, and where, by a third coincidence, a photographer had taken his picture and displayed it in the camera store window. When Tarden explains to his superiors how he found the agent, they do not believe him and suspect him of having a secret informer they do not know anything about.[2]

Tarden is immediately sent on a new assignment to Indonesia. When he gets there, he hears that the agent he was meant to meet has been captured. To keep suspicion off himself, he carries through on his cover of being part of a conference of psychiatrists and anthropologists. I have discussed (see Chapter 5) how Tarden makes fun of one of the psychiatrists and is attacked by the psychiatrist's wife, into whose dormitory he creeps at night, and threatening that he will murder her husband with his deadly poison ring, makes her accept his sexual advances.

At the end of the conference, all are lined up to board the airplane to take them back to their home countries. Suddenly the police arrive. Tarden, believing he is about to be captured, and probably tortured, brings up his poison ring to commit suicide. Not realizing what is going on, the woman he had violated, wanting to get back at him in some way, suddenly knocks him down, pretending it was an accident. At that moment, the police get out and merely direct the traffic of the passengers into the plane. Her action of intended revenge, by sheer chance, had saved Tarden's life.

In *Blind Date,* chance and coincidence become major themes. In the beginning, Levanter hears a woman, Pauline, playing a piece on the piano that his mother used to play. He meets her, and it turns out that Pauline had the same teacher his mother did. When he says the teacher was his mother's mistress, Pauline suggests that she also was the teacher's mistress, creating a connection between them. The connection is increased when it turns out Levanter and his mother have been lovers. He and Pauline lose touch with one another; but at the end of the novel, by sheer chance Levanter sees her name on a poster, hears her play, and they come together as lovers, completing the connection suggested at the beginning.

Then there is the episode, already reported, in which young Levanter, at camp, uses another's techniques to rape a girl he admires. By coincidence, he meets the girl the next year, they hit it off, and are on the point of becoming lovers. But he unconsciously kisses her in the way the rapist had, and she realizes it was him, and leaves him in a rage.[3]

Coincidence as Plot

We would be patronizing of such pat, often almost sentimental coincidences in a nineteenth-century Victorian novel. But with Kosinski, who is so sternly opposed to the falsifications of life suggested by any sort of conventional plot, we realize that he is making a philosophical point. Kosinski rejects a conventional plot because, by making us look ahead to the "foreshadowed" conclusion, it seduces us away from looking at the incident before our eyes at the present moment, which is where our actual life takes place. Though coincidence, oddly, creates something like a plot in *Blind Date,* it is a plot of blind chance, of "blind dates," and so once more reminds us that the future is out of our hands, that only the present exists as an arena for our exertions.

Jacques Monod was in real life a friend of Kosinski's, and Kosinski now imports him into the novel. Levanter and Monod one day are discussing Levanter's friend Romarkin. Monod observes "Romarkin doesn't dare to admit that blind chance and nothing else is responsible for each random event of his life. Instead, he is searching for a religion that, like Marxism, will assure him that man's destiny is spelled out in the central plot of life. Meanwhile, believing in the existence of an orderly, predetermined life scheme, Romarkin bypasses the drama of each unique instance of his own existence. Yet, to accept a notion of destiny, he might as well believe in astrology, or palm reading, or pulp novels, all of which pretend that one's future is already set and needs only to be lived out" (86).

Dasein

Though Kosinski puts these words into the mouth of a "real" person, we easily see that they express the underlying philosophy of all the novels we have thus far examined. Kosinski has said that *Chance and Necessity* is a book which has greatly influenced him. But an equally great influence, I believe, is a book by the German philosopher Martin Heidegger called *Being and Time* (1927).

Dasein, a word Kosinski is fond of (it was the working title of *Being There*[4]), is the term Heidegger uses to refer to Being, or self-hood. The important question for Heidegger—as for Kosinski's protagonists—is the quest for being. The *being* constitutes three fundamental aspects: (1) Facticity: we are already in a world not of our making; (2) Existentiality: the act of making my world mine—"Being exists as anticipation of its own possibilities: it exists in advance of itself and grasps its situation as a challenge to its own power of becoming what it may, rather than being what it must be"; (3) Forfeiture: the scattering of our essential forward drive through attention to the distracting and disturbing cares of everyday and of the things and people that surround us everyday. Thus, inevitably and continuously, the forward-driving *I* is sacrificed to the persistent and pressing *they.* "If the world is material for our creative energy, it is also the agent by which we are seduced from the essential drive to understand and to create."

What rescues us from forfeiture—the daily routine—and makes us grasp our own being, is dread *(Angst),* our sense of our coming death. We authenticate ourselves by recognizing our one unique action, which is our own death. We see our whole self only when we see our past and future (i.e., death) and how they both create the present moment.[5]

The idea of using the fear, or at any rate the complete awareness of approaching death, to push aside the daily routine in order to live and experience fully the present moment is basic in all of Kosinski's writing. An obvious early example would be the young boy in *The Painted Bird* lying between the rails while the train thundered overhead. "I felt life within me as pure as milk. . . . Nothing mattered except the simple fact of being alive" (198).

With Tarden in *Cockpit,* and Levanter in *Blind Date,* the fact that they are aging, and the fact that they cannot trust the erratic rhythms of their hearts ("if the crude, simple pump falters . . . [Levanter] could do nothing more than react with intense terror" [30]), both serve as pointers that they are keeping their mortality present in their minds.

Contra Chance

If Facticity—the world we must live in, the body we must inhabit—is a product of pure chance, as Monod scientifically demonstrates to us, a question arises. Supposing that with our *Angst,* or "terror," our awareness of our limited and finite future, we are *able* to shove aside the soothing seductions of religion, society, television, which all insist that death only happens to the other guy—supposing we are *able* to concentrate on the present moment, then: how do we existentially create our being, fulfill our possibility, seize control of that part of our life over which we can exercize some control? *Blind Date* provides examples for us to examine.

First, there is the Foxy Lady, a beautiful young girl the protagonist has an exciting sexual affair with—until he learns she is actually a man who just had a sex-change operation. The given world she was presented with by fate was to have a functionally male body, but the drives and hormonal system of a female, which made him/her develop breasts and an uncertain sexual identity. Though born in a Moslem country where males are all-important, and females are chattel, the Foxy Lady has decided to take her ambiguous destiny into her hands and create herself a female, at least superficially. "And they say only secret agents live in disguise!" (148) she says bitterly, at the same time that she seems to be aligning herself with other marginal Kosinski characters.

The cost to her is great. She is disowned by her wealthy and powerful father, who is able to have her passport revoked, so that she becomes a citizen of no country (Levanter, pointedly enough, had met her in the "no-man's land" between two countries), has cut herself off, really, from having a normal role in either sex, and even, with her amputation, seems to have lost her ability to have orgasm. It is not easy, obviously, to choose for yourself, rather than going along with society. And for *Angst,* she need only go upstairs to a special room in the private club she and her kind resort to. There are the middle-aged transsexuals, looking aged and coarse and bloated from hormone overdoses, their sex drive gone, their looks vanished, sleeping most of the time, and staying drugged.

Her choice is made, and now she must perforce live her entire life in the present moment, for sex, for dancing, for being admired for her startling beauty by all the men around. "And for what? For no more than a short appearance just for them. Until I end up upstairs too!" (151)

On the other hand, had she opted for the easy way—the sham role of male—she would have had wealth and social acceptance, but not even the brief life of fulfillment of the Foxy Lady.

Another woman Levanter meets is as singularly blasted by her given fate as could be imagined. She is twenty-six years old, but a bone disease she had contracted as a child had left her terribly deformed. She has no legs, an infant-sized body, and brief, stiff, toadlike appendages for arms. Her head is normal-sized, expressive, and quite beautiful. A nurse takes her around in a baby pram.

Rather than letting fate crush her, she is living a rewarding life, attending a university to study art history. She has learned four foreign languages, has a boyfriend she is emotionally committed to, and, most amazingly, spends her holidays hitchhiking about Europe. "Each summer a friend takes me to the main highway and thumbs a ride for me," she explains. Of course, I always have money and my papers with me. Eventually, someone—a man or woman, a couple, or even a family—comes along who does not mind picking me up. After that, I'm on my own—passed from hand to hand, from car to car" (190).

This woman is actually one more of the large number of real people Kosinski has put in *Blind Date.*[6]

Another real-life character has a position in the philosophical scheme of the novel. When Levanter meets biologist and philosophical writer Jacques Monod, Monod is dying of leukemia. Monod has clearly outlined the given world, a world of indifference, a world in which we cannot take shelter behind the false assurances of society or religion, a world in which we must make our own meaning, always with the knowledge that sheer chance, in the form of leukemia, perhaps, might strike us down at any moment.

When Levanter meets him, the disease has reached a point where only frequent transfusions are keeping him alive. Nonetheless, he proposes a lengthy trip out of the city. "Why won't you remain in Paris?" Levanter asks him. "All the life-support equipment is here." But Monod, having accepted the fate which chance has dealt him, is sufficiently master of himself that he prefers to live, and die, with dignity. "'To be hooked up to life through a machine?' he asked abruptly. 'The flame isn't worth the candle'" (87).

Levanter as a Small Investor

Where does Levanter himself fit into the scheme? His "given" is to live in a world of blind chance in which at any moment his heart might stop forever. In other words, his given is exactly the same as ours or any other mortal's—though perhaps he is more aware of it than we are.

How does he behave, then, within the limited and finite world we have all been given, in order to make his brief life meaningful? Well, he calls himself a "small investor," and an "idea man." "Small investors," Levanter defines at one point, are "people who risked their personal energy and means to achieve certain unpredictable ends" (88). He describes intellectuals as idea men: "Intellectuals are our best allies. . . . They invest all their energy and resources in ideas that change man's condition" (34). Levanter's father had once told him that "civilization is the result of sheer chance plus a thousand or two exceptional men and women of ideas and action. . . . Levanter had discovered that . . . all these men and women were, at least at some time in their lives, small investors" (87–88).

Levanter himself most admires a famous plastic surgeon he knows, who with his skill can repair defaced and hideous faces and bodies: "Levanter spent hours in this operating theater, elated, curious, fascinated, watching the surgeon respond to physical reality. His friend's investment required no explanation; the motive was implicit in the result, and the result was obvious for everyone to see: the defeat of blind nature by rational man" (183).

Quite clearly, then, there is a social dimension to the fully authentic man. Not only must he make his own life rewarding, but he must as well make life better for those around him. Certainly this attitude is a change from those of the selfish protagonists of the earlier novels, although we noted that Tarden, in *Cockpit*, takes a step in this direction. Let me quote again Kosinski's words: "My protagonists do not isolate themselves. They are adventurers but also self-appointed reformers of an unjust world: they interfere on behalf of the weak and the fallen and the disfigured. I see this as an important part of the philosophy of the self: you cannot be faithful to your own sense of drama if you disregard the drama in the life of others—those right next to you."[7]

We have seen Levanter in his acts of impersonal justice against the minister of internal affairs, against the desk-clerk informer. In other scenes we see him acting to release political prisoners in totalitarian countries. There is a brief epigraph from Jacques Monod at the beginning of the novel on the fact that man must determine his own morals.

Let me give here the entire passage from which the epigraph is taken, as it will cast light on Levanter's actions: "Now does [post-scientific man] at last realize that, like a gypsy, he lives on the boundary of an alien world. A world that is deaf to his music, just as indifferent to his hopes as it is to his suffering or his crimes. But henceforth who is to define crime? Who shall decide what is good and what is evil? All the traditional systems have placed ethics and values beyond man's reach. Values did not belong to him; he belonged to them. He now knows that they are his and his alone, and they no sooner come into his possession than lo! they seem to melt into the world's uncaring emptiness."[8]

Moral decisions are transient, he seems to be saying, because they must be made from moment to moment, in the face of the chance events just then impinging. The speed with which each moral act "melts" away perhaps explains why Levanter, after committing his acts of justice, so quickly feels "removed" (38) from them.

Love

On the personal level, Levanter attempts to make his life meaningful from moment to moment in some of the standard ways past Kosinski protagonists have used, skiing dangerous slopes, putting himself in the way of adventures with new people in new places. But there is significant change from earlier novels. He is a softened, more human, more compassionate protagonist, less interested in personal revenge, less interested in controlling other human beings. Sex, in *Blind Date,* is less a battle than it has been in previous novels, less an act of aggression. The possibility, at least, of love seems present.

Tarden, in *Cockpit,* was capable of forcing his sexual attention on a woman just because she had behaved hostilely toward him, and indeed, later in the novel he murders a woman who will not let him force his attentions on her.

We see Levanter almost in a transitional position. For as a young man, following Oscar's directions, he quite brutally rapes a girl at summer camp. Had this episode been in *Cockpit,* we would simply have gone on to the next episode, with never a glance back. The consequences in *Blind Date* are quite different, and it is worth looking at the entire episode of the rape closely.

When Levanter, then fifteen years old, is about to board the train to camp, he drops his suitcase onto the tracks under the train. The train is about to start. He hesitates to jump down. Suddenly a boy next to him jumps down, rescues the suitcase, and climbs up an instant before the train starts.

This is Oscar, just such an adventurer with life as would be attractive to a Kosinski protagonist. He admires the boy greatly—"If Levanter could have magically changed his appearance, he would have wanted to look exactly like Oscar" (60)—and so listens perhaps more receptively than he might have when Oscar later tells him of his career of raping women. "Breaking their eye" is the special term he uses for it, and "blind dates" are what he called his victims, for since he always takes them from behind, they never see his face. "Blind dating—along with other occasional acts of daring, like crawling under a train seconds before it started moving—was all that interested him in life"(63).

In a way, he is such a protagonist as Kosinski might have put in an earlier novel, and so it is perhaps no wonder that young Levanter is attracted to him, and actually, for a few brief moments, *becomes* him, when he rapes the young girl himself.

The girl—tall, and with a thick blond braid—is one he had been attracted to from the first time he saw her, but he was too shy ever to speak to her. Too shy to speak, finally he rapes her: "She screamed, and he thought that, without having spoken a single word to her, he had just become her first lover" (67). He ties her hand and foot and further abuses her before releasing her. He is bothered that, not wanting her to see his face and be able to identify him, he has not been able to see her face either, to see what emotion was in her eyes.

The next spring he meets her—scarcely recognizing her at first because the thick blond braid has been cut. They see a lot of each other, but he is still shy of speech with her. He does not want to know her name, but calls her "Nameless," instead. He is constantly worried that she will find out about him. "I am afraid of losing you, Nameless. Of losing you again" (75). At the moment they are about to become lovers, she suddenly realizes he is the one who had raped her, and leaves him at once. And it seems that Levanter has missed a real opportunity.

I have said that, too shy to speak to the girl, he had raped her. If love is to be more than simply one person controlling another, which is to say, if it is to be more than a kind of rape, there must be communication. Communication is what the young boy in *The Painted Bird* finally withheld from the rest of the world when it went beyond certain bounds in its cruelty to him. In one passage we learn that Levanter, too, like that boy, was briefly mute as a result of the war (93). Language, as a form of necessary communication between lovers, becomes a complex issue. Levanter, after the episode with the girl, becomes his mother's lover, and their relationship goes on for years. But oddly, they never speak about it. "Her bed was like a silent, physical confessional: what happened between them there was never talked about" (10). Later he meets a beautiful Russian actress, but is unable to carry through on his seduction of her, feeling hopelessly inhibited by his Russian language. Oscar, perhaps to escape the same sort of language inhibition, invents his own vocabulary of blind dates and breaking eyes.

Kosinski has said that "most of us by the time of adolescence, carry in our head a veritable totalitarian state of illusions and most of them suppress us. Take the sexual areas:. . . . The two lovers on the solitary lover's lane more often talk and answer to their inner censors than to each other." And speaking of the sense of liberation he feels writing in his adopted English, he has said "It seemed that the languages of my childhood and adolescence—Polish and Russian—carried a sort of mental suppression."[9]

Music as Language

But his mother had another way of communicating with him: through her music. There is no hint in the novel that their sexual relationship was not perfectly fulfilling. It is music, the same piece that his mother used to play on the piano, that first brings him together with Pauline. She is playing the same piece again when he rediscovers her at the end of the novel.

Once more, the scene must be examined closely.

As he listens, the music is "pure spirit without words, without gestures." There is communication nonetheless. But, sitting near the back of the hall "he could hardly see the pianist's features and seemed to be looking at her through the wrong end of the opera glasses" (226).[10] At the end of the performance he goes to her dressing room, then invites her to his apartment. She wants to know why. "'I'm afraid of losing you,' he said. The sound of his words brought him a faint memory, so faint that he dismissed it." They are, of course, the words he had used with Nameless, the girl he had raped. "I want you to fall in love with me," he tells her, and then, in this novel of chance, says, "Somehow, I think you're my last chance" (227).

They begin to make love—records of her piano playing on the phonograph—but somehow she cannot give herself up to him, cannot surrender. Time and again as she is about to reach her climax she pulls back. "I can't," she said, "I never could" (229).

But by this time Levanter has seen what is beginning to dawn on the alert reader (who, checking back to Levanter's first sight of Pauline, at the beginning of the novel, finds that she does indeed have "thick blond hair" [8]), that the novel's biggest chance coincidence has come round to bring the novel full circle. He now takes an armful of neckties from his closet (this time the softest, smoothest he has) and gently, but convincingly, ties her hand and foot (as he had tied her in the woods thirty years before), recreating the scene, but gently this time, with her permission, and face to face, and "heard her whisper, 'Yes!' and, as its sound ebbed, her body softened, freed from its own bondage, no longer struggling against any restraints" (231).

The personal violence against others symbolized in his original binding and raping of the girl, has been sublimated into social action; the binding and raping (with the saber, or *rapier*) of the desk-clerk informer—leaving him free for the gentle, psychotherapeutic binding and raping of Pauline in love.

Memory and the Spontaneous

Kosinski tries, in the scene, to bring some sort of resolution to another aesthetic/philosophical problem. Memory, as we have seen in our discussion of earlier novels, is both a help and a hindrance in living our lives fully and richly. Memory of the past can trap us, make us an object of history, rather than a subject of the present moment. Pauline, for instance, has been made an object of the rape in her childhood, which has stopped her from having sexual fulfillment. But when

Levanter recreates the binding, the rape, in a way he is using the memory of past trauma to heal, to bring her to living in and responding to the present act.

Using his own memory of the past traumatic act to recreate it in the present is essentially what the novelist does when he takes the ingredients of his past to create his fictions. Through her art, her piano playing, Pauline is able to take Levanter back to his original meeting with her, just as at that original meeting she took him back to memory of his mother. When he first met her, he told her an odd story about a baseball player. When she sees him again, at the end of the novel, the first thing she thinks of is that story. "You told me about him for a reason. What was it?" "I hoped you would remember the story. And possibly remember the person who told it to you" (227). He had listened to her play in her concert and compliments her afterwards. "A good audience," she says, "But the audience is gone now. All that's left is the recording, a memory." "But it's a memory with feeling, which can be listened to many times," Levanter comes back at her. (There is an obvious analogy with the printed novel.) She agrees, "But only as a source of reflection; no more magic of the spontaneous" (226).

In his personal relationship with her, Levanter wants the "spontaneous magic" (228). Memory is not enough. Even memory with feeling is second to living in the actual present moment. So life is better than art—but, and here is the point: art can bring us to the present moment, by reminding us, by shocking us, into the *Angst* needed. In this sense, Kosinski does not separate memory from the imagination: "I think you start by imagining yourself in the very situation which frightens you. Hence, the enormous importance of imagination, our ability to project oneself into the 'unknown'—the very 'blind dates' of our existence. For instance, you are in the midst of playing tennis and suddenly you see yourself as not being able to play it ever again—a victim of a car accident, a crippling disease, old age. . . . In the moment of such a projection you are at peace with both your own condition and with a change this condition implies. . . . You intensify your joy of the moment . . . and you ready yourself for whatever might be, for the innumerable contingencies you might have to face in your life."[11]

Authentication

If *Blind Date* then ended, with their coming together in the present moment—as a novel of conventional plot and coincidence would end—it would be false to Kosinski's imaginative vision of the contingencies we must bear in mind in order to enjoy our spontaneous moments fully. Instead the novel concludes in the only way that it truthfully can, with the most inescapable fact of our life, which is our death.

Levanter is on the ski slopes, and descending is like his whole life in little: "A descent was like life: to love it was to love each moment, to rejoice in the skill and speed of every moment. Soon, skiing down these fields, he would appropriate them as if they had been set there just for him, to be fleetingly possessed, the possession vanishing an instant after it took place" (231).

Though it is late in the season, spring approaching, cold weather catches him by surprise and without adequate clothing. He is lost in the fog, and though he fights against it, slowly the cold is claiming him. "He had been scoring quite well in the games he played. . . . The game was good to him, made him want to play it, yet even a solitary player needs his rest. . . . He sank down and turned his face away from the wind" (235).

Autobiographical Elements in *Blind Date*

In the preceding discussion, through analyzing scenes, through arranging episodes into thematic sequences, through tying together scattered references, and especially, through suggesting the novel's philosophical framework, I have tried to show that *Blind Date* marks a distinct shifting away from the violence and cruelty and egoistic protagonists of Kosinski's previous novels, and towards a gentler and more human protagonist, and an opening for the possibility of love.

But if careful analysis can reveal these benign tendencies, I well remember that my first reading of the novel did not immediately show them to me. I recall my shock at the rape of the girl at the summer camp, and my feeling of disappointment at the following scene of Levanter meeting the girl the next spring, falling in love with her and then losing her. I read it as a dangerous lapse into sentimentality and was put off by the too pat coincidence. Now that I understand the novel better, I do not respond in that way.

I was most especially disturbed, in my first reading, by something else Kosinski did. He put into the novel several persons from real life, persons he knows or has met. The technique has been used before in other novels by other writers. But what Kosinski did was to present these real people in embarrassing or unhappy and finally in tragic situations, Monod dying of leukemia, and old and tired Charles Lindbergh—with Levanter asking him unpleasant questions about Lindbergh's seeming support of the Nazis, a character very close to his own wife dying of a brain tumor, and, ugliest of all, the long, nightmarish recreation of the Manson gang murdering people who, in real life, were close friends of Kosinski's on a night when he was meant to be in the house himself.

It seemed to me like bad taste, and it was difficult not to feel Kosinski was exploiting for the sake of his fiction tragedy that had touched his closest friends.

At the same time I could not deny that these very scenes constituted some of the most powerful fiction I have read recently. As, indeed, with other powerful scenes in all of Kosinski's novels, the reader was confronted with a powerful fictional construction which also had the backing of real life as a felt presence behind it.

Once more, there is a philosophical justification for what Kosinski has done. According to Kosinski's aesthetic, popular culture, television, commercial fiction, our social and religious and political institutions are designed to dull our awareness of the pain and death everywhere waiting to claim us. Because we are lulled we do not live our lives fully, we do not sufficiently appreciate every moment. The purpose of art, Kosinski believes, is to shock us into awareness of our danger, for the salutary purpose of making us appreciate what we have, the brief, chancy, but inestimable privilege of life. His aesthetic accords, once more, with Heidegger, whose concept of "forfeiture" is precisely that the routine of everydayness seduces us from authentic life, which only the shock of *Angst* can save us from. Heidegger indeed sees art as one of the methods for rescuing us. "Through poetry," he believes, "we may hope, perhaps, to recover that 'illumination of being' from which we have so long gone astray."[12]

Blind Date as Spiritual Autobiography

Blind Date has as many or more fragments of actual autobiography in it as any Kosinski novel. Levanter, as young boy just after the war, was mute and anti-social; he has a young pianist mother, a much older father who has retired from life to study philology. His background is Russian and Polish. He is a photographer in an eastern European country. He defects to America. He meets, through one of his publications, a wealthy woman whom he then marries and lives with till she dies of a brain tumor. He narrowly misses being murdered by the Manson gang at Sharon Tate's house. He meets Svetlana Stalin while he is a lecturer at Princeton, and so on. We have seen that these "quotations" from real life are frequent in Kosinski's novels. But I have suggested (see Chapter 6) that in *Cockpit* Kosinski was beginning, in a symbolical way, not only to use the stuff of his life in his novels, but to make his protagonist an embodiment of himself, though disguised in various ways.

The tendency is carried further in *Blind Date.* For Levanter's "small investor" and "idea man" we need only read "novelist." The investment is the investment of life, and Levanter's publications are concerned with the effects of chance on investments. It is through his writing that he meets his wife, that he makes his living, and so on. Crucially important is the social consciousness, the making use of his position as small investor to attack totalitarianism, the use of his art and his talents to free political prisoners (as in the scene where he trades photographs of some dignitaries of a foreign country for political prisoners they hold). Levanter is president of Investor's International—a body obviously close to P.E.N., which Kosinski was president of, and which works to free writers and intellectuals held as political prisoners.

In beginning to deal with himself as disguised protagonist of his novel, Kosinski, as we have noted, is moving away from protagonists who represent extreme, desperate positions, to more moderate, more humanly vulnerable, but also more successful protagonists. He has written several novels to point out the dangers and difficulties of life, but having personally been through many of the most traumatic upheavals and disruptions of our recent desperate history, he is in all senses a survivor. He has come through, and he has triumphed. More than most others, he is in a position to be an example to us.

Chapter Eight
Passion Play

Passion Play carries much further the tendencies first noted in *Cockpit* and extended in *Blind Date*. Fabian, the protagonist, is older, more vulnerable, less vengeful. The comedy in the novel is quieter, more sophisticated, more in the language than the action. If Levanter, in *Blind Date,* operated on an international scale, trying to make the world slightly better by eliminating those tyrants who would enslave us, Fabian is more parochial. As he says of himself, he is strictly a one-on-one man; and if he improves the world, it is not by eliminating the enslavers, but rather by freeing to their full potential the individuals—in this case the young ladies he trains in "horsemanship."

Passion Play, which continues the spiritual biography of Kosinski himself, is a more romantic, more sentimental book than the earlier novels, and is, in structure, more conventionally plotted. The language is lusher—perhaps too lush in places. In spite of these changes or developments, the novel remains very distinctly a Kosinski novel.

Passion Play

Fabian is a polo player who writes books about what it means to be a rider. He lives in his VanHome, a motor home with room for his two horses in the back. He has never been a team man: he makes his living playing one-on-one for stakes. Also he makes a small amount of money from his books, from lecturing, and from training young girls in horsemanship as he travels about the country.

It is a poor living, and from day to day he does not know if he will have enough money to feed his horses or drive his VanHome. Also, he is growing older, hair thinning and turning gray, teeth loosening, recurrent back trouble.

He appears distinctly anachronistic when, having driven into the city at night, he takes his horses out on a deserted downtown parking lot to practice polo. The image of the gaunt, ridiculous, yet somehow noble Don Quixote is never far away.

When in the past he had played on teams, he had never shared the ball, but had scored only for himself. When other players crossed him, he went for them directly, and they were sometimes hurt in "accidents." So he has been more or less blackballed from any but his favorite one-on-one challenges.

For a while he had been a friend and sort of paid partner to Eugene Stanhope, a millionaire who played polo as a hobby. But then Fabian had been seduced one night by Stanhope's girl friend Alexandra. The next day Alexandra claimed that Fabian had attempted to force himself on her, and she had had to run out. Stanhope, in a fury, had challenged Fabian to a one-on-one match, but in the match it became clear that Stanhope was going directly for Fabian, to try to murder him. With a fluke hit, Fabian drove the ball into Stanhope's head, killing him.

A few years later Alexandra has her new boyfriend, a rich South American professional polo player, challenge Fabian for money. She appears to want to humiliate Fabian. Fabian gets together as much money as he has to bet against the South American. The South American is injured in the rough play and has to concede defeat.

At another time in his past he was, similarly, a paid partner and friend of the Trujillo-like dictator of a country in the Caribbean. His job is to make the dictator look young and virile in carefully orchestrated and filmed polo matches. But when Fabian finds himself being used in the dictator's plot to eliminate an outspoken journalist, he leaves.

As a teacher of horsemanship, Fabian prefers to teach beautiful high-school-age girls who have an aptitude for the sport. He not only teaches them riding, but initiates them sexually. The training in riding and in sex follow similar philosophies (and are described in similar vocabulary). In both, Fabian aims to bring out the total potential in his students.

His best student was Vanessa Stanhope, niece of the Stanhope who had died in the match with him. She is his readiest and most talented learner in both his fields of instruction. But because she is a minor, and he does not want to be caught and charged with statutory rape, they carefully preserve her technical virginity, doing everything they can think of sexually, but always preserving her hymen.

Now, years, later, he comes back to claim what he had not taken. She is grown now, a beautiful and extremely wealthy heiress, in the prime of her youth. He is old and gaunt—older than her father, almost penniless, and desperately in need of a job. She has remained a virgin for him; and when he hesitates, she literally forces herself on him, using him to launch her into womanhood.

She is the one person he has really loved; and perhaps he has avoided all these years the final sexual consummation, because, once having finally launched her into life, he would feel he had fulfilled his role as teacher and would then have to move on. He had not wanted to lose her finally, but now he prepares to leave.

She does all she can to keep him, even presenting him with a no-strings-attached gift of $1 million, so that he will be independent, and money will not come between them.

But he recognizes that what she is asking for is a kind of possession of him, a robbing him of the stern independence and solitude of his nomadic life. He refuses her gift, and leaves.

The Will and the Flesh

The horses in the novel are genuine horses, of course, nicely and convincingly realized. But they appear to have a symbolical dimension as well, representing the body, as the rider represents the will or spirit. The idea of horse and rider being a single entity is suggested, for instance, by the names of the two polo teams Fabian watches, the "Centauros," and the "Hybrids" (39).[1]

He speaks first, of his actual body, as a thing subject to him, but with its own autonomous life as well: observing in the mirror the decay of his body through age, "Fabian saw his spirit as remote from his body. His attempts at mechanical perfection, his horsemanship, his polo, were acts of violence committed by the spirit against an unwilling, submissive body. But now, his body, once only the expression of his spirit, had become a form for aging, nature's own expression" (12).

He speaks of his horses in similar terms: "the union of rider and mount was, at base, a duel of human brain and animal physiology." He then describes the horse in purely mechanistic terms, "a self-propelled crane," a "mobile suspension bridge," and so on. "But just as those sophisticated devices were vulnerable to misuse, so, too, any horse, however skilfully trained, might, when pushed beyond the limits of its physiology by a rider's will, collapse" (24–25).

The horse—and therefore by extension his own body—appears to remain for him at the level of mechanism. The horse is never "he" or "she" but always "it." He contrasts a New Zealand polo team with a South American team. All the players on the New Zealand team are rated identically at nine (ten is the best rating possible). After a tournament anywhere in the world, the New Zealanders bear the expense of bringing their horses home with them. The crowd likes them, likes their "link to an Anglo-Saxon legacy of respecting the horse." The South American team, on the other hand, has two ten-rated players, and two eights, and they sell their ponies at auction after the match. They "never staked winning on one horse" but used several in a match, training them mainly for speed, using drugs to stimulate them and anesthetics to keep them from noticing pain. The New Zealander, "even at the game's hottest pitch . . . spurred his pony more by the pressure of knees and calves than by punishing it with whip," whereas the South American, with his "peculiar vehemence of temperament . . . whipped his pony, flanks already bloodied, into a frenzied gallop" (45).

These qualities turn the crowd against them, but it is for just these reasons Fabian prefers them, preferring the single star rather than the even team, and preferring to drive horse and body fiercely and passionately to their greatest heights.

On the other hand, if the mastery he demands over his horse, and over his own body, is severe, even brutal, it is directed toward bringing out the true potential of that horse, and of his body.

The point is brought out in his relationship with Stella. Stella, when he begins teaching her, appears to be a typical blonde Southern Belle. She is training her horse to win dressage competitions with its several very elaborate gaits. She claims that the horse is bred to these gaits, has an actual inclination to walk in these various artificial manners. But when we see her training the horse, we learn that in fact she rigs it with complicated weights and braces that virtually cripple the horse into moving in a very unnatural manner. Fabian accuses her of treating her horse exactly as the Southern masters used to treat their slaves, forcing their wills to unnatural bondage (160).

The point becomes clearer when Fabian, who had been unable to get anywhere with Stella sexually, searches into her closely and suddenly realizes that, though she had forced her body unnaturally into the mold of a Southern Belle, in truth she is a black herself, a beautiful albino.

Now she comes to him sexually, because, thanks to him, "I am myself. Finally myself" (165), and we later see her married to a black civil-rights attorney. In the meantime, however, she sells her horse to Fabian for a third its market price, and he retrains it for polo, a sport that brings out the horse's true attributes.

Training Them Young

Just as there is an advantage, in horse training, to finding your horse while it is still young, before it has possibly been mistrained by another, so Fabian, in training young ladies in horsemanship, prefers them high-school age and virgin. The training, which is designed to free them into being their most essential selves, is carried on sexually, but the analogies between training horses and training young virgins are kept very close. And, a surprise in a Kosinski work, the analogies are often handled quite humorously.

The story of an older man devoting himself to the pursuit of teen-agers immediately suggests Humbert Humbert's pursuit of "nymphets" in Vladimir Nabokov's *Lolita*. The humor Kosinski employs is also Nabokovian in its playfulness. Puns on the genus *Equus* abound. For instance, when Fabian is out to take Stella's virginity, he tells us he would like "to break her equanimity" (161). As the young girls in lepidopterist Nabokov's books are sometimes described in terms reminiscent of butterflies, the young girls in *Passion Play* are described in what the alerted reader can see are horselike terms. The women he preferred were "young, tall, slender, long-legged, with large eyes and thick hair, a wide mouth" (110). In Vanessa, we are adverted to "the expressive eyes, high cheekbones, lush hair, the wide mouth, even teeth." Indeed, "accenting her mouth was a deep cleft in her upper lip, a scar that invited speculation about her" (194). We see Alexandra's "mane of copper-colored hair" (52) and are told she has a "broad mobile mouth, framing wide teeth" (68). There is even the suggestion of a horse's gait when he describes Stella's converation, "her aloof manner, the languid rise and fall of her speech" (164).

He finds the young girls he pursues by thumbing through the pages of the *Saddle Bride,* a trade journal of the horse world. Within he finds glossy pictures of debutantes of the horse set, with all their best points listed, almost as if they were horses to be offered to the highest bidder, but also almost like one of those catalogues that swinging singles clubs use to match up their members. The double-entendre of the title of the journal, suggesting a play on horseback riding and sexual intercourse, is exploited fully. Among other details of the young girls, we are told the names of their "favorite mounts." Of Stella, for instance, we learn she was given a championship award in the "Plantation Pleasure competition" and was also accomplished in the "Breeders Futurity event for young riders" (156).

When he is teaching the girls "horsemanship" the analogy between teaching girls and training horses is explicit: Fabian tells us he wishes to put his "brand" (139) on the young high-school girls. He knows that "just as he should not expect a pony to bend to the curb, to the rein and spur without prior schooling and cultivation, neither should he expect a young woman . . . to come to him" (138). "He knew that if Vanessa were to come to him as he willed, it must be to imprint him in her memory; like a colt, she was to be schooled, he at the lead, she following at liberty, without rigs, harness, reins" (196). These are a few of numerous examples.

When they make love, there are of course numerous plays on mounting and so on. These come to their fullest expression when he is with Stella, as sometimes he would make love to her wearing spurs, at another he would put bridles and other gear on her, at another he would press her up against a horse's backside, and take her there, as if he were actually mating with the horse (165ff.).

As in earlier Kosinski novels, the purpose is to take away the last of the girls' inhibitions, to free them from their restraint-filled past, to bring out the fullness of their being, and make them live solidly in the sensation of the moment. A part of the intensity is the fact that the moment is transitory, that he is a nomad who will leave them the moment he has found them. The moment will gain in importance for being nonrepeatable. If he stayed with them, they would fall into habit and routine, and the moment would be smothered, buried under past recollections, and lacking the *Angst* of imminent departure.

Ambiguous Situations

But human relationships can be perilous. If conducted properly, they are mutually liberating. On the other hand, one person, fearful of making himself vulnerable, can instead try to master the other, to become subject by destroying the other's selfhood and making him an object.

We are told of Fabian that "he had acted always on the conviction that to master his life, to assert dominion over that indifferent span, what he must do was to shape it into drama, each scene so charged, so unrepeatable, that no interval could be permitted to divert him from the spectacle of which he was both protagonist and solitary witness" (71). As itinerant polo player, penniless professional in a sport of millionaires, part of his drama is constantly to risk himself in personal relationships. At least two of these are extremely ambiguous.

For some time he is a paid friend and polo partner to Falsalfa, the Trujillo-like dictator of a Caribbean island. Under the partnership Fabian has no further financial worries, living in one or another sumptuous villa, fine horses and skilled grooms at his beck. His only responsibility is to set up carefully rehearsed polo matches to be filmed for newsreels, which show the aging dictator to be vigorous and agile, outplaying everyone on the field.

During a lavish weekend party at the dictator's estate, Fabian meets a young woman and is at once attracted to her. She turns out to be the devoted wife of a much older man, a journalist well known for being the only one who dares to be critical of the regime. Falsalfa is forced to tolerate him because of international pressure. Fabian had invited the man and his wife to take a horseback ride into the jungle interior with him. They had both begged off, having no interest in the trip, but Falsalfa, overhearing, at once insists that they go, and they cannot get out of it.

The two guides who accompany them are carrying submachine guns, and Fabian suspects they are the dictator's henchmen. The ride is hot, longer than they expected, grueling, the aging journalist falls from his horse and is injured. At last they arrive at a primitive village. The natives insist that they sample the local drink. Fabian goes into a dreamlike state where at one time the journalist's young wife seems to be dancing lasciviously before him, at aother moment the journalist is attacking him with a machete, at another Fabian is on the floor making love to the woman, with dozens of natives looking on.

In the morning the journalist is dead, his wife heavily sedated and unconscious. One of Falsalfa's henchmen claims he was killed by the bite of a tarantula. Fabian knows that somehow Falsalfa has had him killed, but when he charges the dictator with the crime, he merely laughs at Fabian, reminding him that dozens of witnesses saw him making love to the journalist's wife, and the journalist fighting with him. If there is an investigation, any court would find Fabian guilty. Fabian cannot deny it, nor can he deny what seem to have been his own actions, though he feels he was somehow drugged.

He is being used in the most obvious way, being made an object by Falsalfa. A careful reading of the dreamlike scene (103–104) suggests that, drugged, he was indeed maneuvered into the girl's arms. But he did in fact make love with her, though had his mind been clear, he would not have wanted, perhaps, to come between the man and his wife.

The scene spells out the falsity of his whole relationship with the dictator, suggested already by the name Falsalfa. By denying his own strong perfectionist drive to win at polo, Fabian had gained in return financial security and luxurious surroundings. But now having it brought home to him how he has lost his freedom of action, he quickly departs the island.[2]

With Eugene Stanhope he has a more subtle, but actually similar relationship. The millionaire Stanhope helps him finance his VanHome and buy his horse, and though the relationship is ostensibly one of friendship, he keeps Fabian virtually as a salaried hand. It is less demeaning; he can play to win, but still it is a kind of bondage. One day Stanhope's beautiful young girl friend, Alexandra, enters the VanHome and seduces Fabian. First she had aroused him by parading her body before him. With her long legs and arms constantly in motion, she tells him the people she works with as a model have nicknamed her the "centipede," suggesting, perhaps, the tarantula of the earlier incident. The next morning, quite inexplicably, she tells Stanhope that Fabian had attempted to force himself on her, and she had had to run from him. It is then that Stanhope challenges Fabian to the one-on-one match in which Stanhope is killed.

Once more, Fabian has been, for the sake of brief financial stability, almost completely in the hands of others.

Vanessa

Of his many young trainees, Vanessa Stanhope (niece of Eugene) is the most important to him.[3] He had discovered her by his usual means of finding her picture in the *Saddle Bride*—where she was advertised as "an honor student" (194). Almost at once she comes to him with great warmth. But because she is underage, and Fabian is worried about being charged with statutory rape if they are caught together and she can be medically proved not to be a virgin, they make it a rule that in all their love-making, no matter what they do they preserve her hymen.

But there is another reason for his refraining from taking her virginity. Fabian, we know, is in a "permanent state of transience" (175). His girls "had to acknowledge that he could offer no more than the union of the night, the courtship of a weekend or the intimacy of a few evenings. . . . He found himself selecting, isolating, soliciting partners as transient and avid as himself, as ready to initiate, as willing to discard" (110-111).

At the moment of "closing in on youth," the events would be for him "counters to the steady waste of time and age that raced between them" and the "relentless flow" in which his age was "a constant subtraction" (138). "Sometimes, after the initiation had been successfully accomplished . . . Fabian's interest in a girl began to wane" (140). And when he would meet one of his trainees in later life, it was no longer the same. He was "aware that the same process of time that had carried her to maturity had made of him a man in midlife" (138).

But Vanessa is from the first moment special to him. "She never ceased to be, for him, sovereign in her possession of a flame of life" (197), that flame always equated, in Kosinski's writing, with that full Heideggerian "being" in the present moment. She is the only one of the girls he has truly loved, and so the preservation of her virginity is in a way an attempt to halt the flow of time, to preserve their relationship in the present moment, to give him a promise to come back to, many years later.

When he does come back to her, towards the end of the novel, he is indeed aging, penniless, his body in decay, while she is in the full bloom of her youth, and, as heiress to the Stanhope fortune, a millionairess many times over. She has kept her virginity for him and now wants him to take it. If it has preserved him from final aging and death, it is holding her back from her full development. He puts off the action for as long as he can, and at the end she must be the one to act: "He stopped, reluctant to name what he felt. Now, when she was willing to resume what he had initiated so long ago, to receive the finality of his mark, to embrace the long arc of his design for her, he saw himself caught in that design" (221). Finally, "she arched both legs . . . and impaled herself on him" (223).

He is left "uncertain whether with each step he was binding her closer to himself or setting her adrift, to shores and reaches of her own" (223).

Alexandra

Quite the most interesting character in the novel is Alexandra, Fabian's curious and ironic nemesis. We see her at three crucial moments in Fabian's life. First, as we have mentioned, she seduces him, then tells Eugene Stanhope that it had been the other way round, initiating the fatal duel between them. Next we see her, a few years later, initiating another challenge match, already described, which would utterly bankrupt Fabian if he lost it; but the young man makes some mistakes in technique that the experienced Fabian uses against him and must concede defeat. The third and last time we see Alexandra, we barely glimpse her. She is little more than a voice in the crowd, shouting at a critical moment in a show-jumping match, when Fabian is trying to jump an extremely tall fence for the championship. Her voice from the past distracts him only a moment; he turns, unbalancing the horse, and the fence is toppled. Fabian loses the match, and nearly takes a bad fall.

Her actions, on the surface, appear to be based on some vicious, inexplicable hatred she has for Fabian. But her complex relationship with Fabian needs to be examined closely.

The first thing to be noted is that everything about her seems to be positive. As with his other girls, she fascinates Fabian from the first moment, and he describes her in the horselike terms of his other girls. When he looks at her, he wonders "who inhabits such a perfect being" (53), and "being" is always a strongly charged plus-word in Kosinski's writing. Their love-making, which is given us in great detail, is complex, and marked by many reversals.

To begin with, it is she who challenges him, and in terms he cannot resist. With the other girls, he had to lure them into his VanHome at first. She demands entrance. "Could it wait for another time?" he asks, hesitating. "It could. But should you?" (52). It is his own ethic she is challenging him with, that the moment, always unrepeatable, must be seized.

In the VanHome, when she invites him to take her, "Fabian felt himself at a crossroad, forced by the will of another to unsettle the harmony he had achieved between his codes and inclinations" (53). It is her will operating, not his. But, "to decline Alexandra's challenge, to thwart his instinct toward her, would ratify an indolence or lapse in value. Either would subvert his trust in himself. . . . The balance of his mind restored" (54), he accepts her challenge.

Even in their love-making, she continues to hold the position that is usually his. In the horse-riding parallels of the scene, we see "her legs upon his chest, her calves girdled around his ribs (56), and we see her insistence on entering all his bodily orifices, and the final bit of control, pulling back and refusing to give him his climax, "knowing that, with orgasm, her power over her lover waned" (57).

But it does not seem to be negative. For she has as well taken over his role as teacher and liberator. First, she keeps him rigidly within the present moment, "commanding his gaze, not allowing him . . . even in thought, to withdraw to another world, one that might be entirely his own—or one that he might share, in recollection or fantasy, with another woman" (56). In their merging, it is finally immaterial to him "what impulses she submitted to in her commitment to his need: whether they were stages in a drama ordered by her and enacted by him, that would permit the revelation of his own nature, his pleasure at the discovery a tribute to her zeal; or whether, provoked by her, he was the one who would disclose what lay hidden in her, what she could not otherwise release, the pleasure she sought most" (57).[4]

Perhaps her withholding orgasm from him in a way parallels his refraining from taking Vanessa's virginity, in both cases a way of extending the moment.

The Centipede and the Tarantula

In the midst of so fruitful a relationship, how, then, explain her treachery to him? In fact, there is no inconsistency.

We have noted that, with her long active hands and arms and legs she has been nicknamed "the centipede" (53). The name is a reminder of that other poisonous arthropod in the novel, the tarantula that appears to have killed the journalist. The parallels are instructive.

Remember that Fabian, working as a hired man for the dictator, was in a false position, in return for financial security faking his polo game to make the dictator look good. The tarantula is what finally adverts him to his position, so that he can at last bring himself to break free of the dictator and leave.

With Eugene Stanhope his position was equally false. Fabian's hesitatioon to take Alexandra at once was a sign of how Eugene had locked him up, subverting his instincts. To be sure, Eugene is not as overtly dictatorial as Falsalfa and, aware that his wealth might give him an unfair advantage over Fabian, as planning to underwrite some manuals on riding with Fabian as editor, "as if to put Fabian on a more independent footing" (53). Alexandra, the centipede, through her seeming treachery, in fact brought on, just as the tarantula had, the necessary rupture between Fabian and Eugene, so that Fabian would once more be true to himself.

When she meets Fabian later, his finances and spirits are at a low ebb. The Stanhope family are offering him a new form of financial security—he can be the television moderator for a series of programs on polo, an attempt to make polo a popular mass-audience sport. Once more it is an unnatural role for him to become spectator, player-at-one-remove, from the real game. But he almost has no choice, with scarcely enough money left to feed his horses. At that moment he meets Alexandra, and she sets up the challenge match with her young boyfriend. It seems as if she is out for revenge, but the upshot is that Fabian makes enough on the match to regain his independence and be able to turn down the television job.

The last meeting between them is the most paradoxical. Fabian has gone to Madison Square Garden to watch the show-jumping competition. Vanessa's horse, Captain Ahab, is competing. But at the last instant, Captain Ahab's rider has a reaction to drugs he had taken to calm him. There is no time to find a replacement. Jumping is not Fabian's sport, but he wants to help Vanessa. He decides to ride the horse himself.

The horse is strong, and he does very well with it. At last all competitors have been eliminated except for Fabian and one other. The other, interestingly, is a woman rider. It is while Fabian is trying to jump a seven-foot fence in the play-off that Alexandra shouts, breaking his concentration, and he loses the match.

Now note that Fabian is in the competition for the sake of Vanessa, who is another of the wealthy Stanhopes. He is a polo player, so in show-jumping he is, for her sake, engaging in a sport unnatural to him. She has, in effect, put the crippling weights and bindings on him that Stella put on her gaited horse. It is significant that the horse he is riding, a horse that is the owned property of Vanessa, is Captain Ahab. Fabian himself is often referred to as a kind of Ahab. Actually in the contest, but symbolically as well, it is a woman he is fighting with for mastery, and the mastery is over himself.

Immediately after the competition, Vanessa offers Fabian a gift of $1 million, taxes paid. Ostensibly, she wants to make him independent, so he can come to her in freedom. It was the same motive Eugene had in offering to underwrite the horsemanship manuals. In practice it would have bound him to her forever.[5]

"Take it, Fabian, take it now!" (241) Alexandra had shouted from the audience. She did not mean, take the jump, win for Vanessa, losing for Captain Ahab. She certainly did not mean take the $1 million and a lifetime of bondage to Vanessa. She meant take your freedom, and take it "now," in the moment, the moment fading, the moment followed no doubt by aging and loneliness and death. But aging and death is the lot of all of us. What makes the difference in life is whether or not we seize our moments of true being.

The Experience of the Novel

My method in the present chapter, and in former chapters, has been to "analyze" the novel, which means, to break it down into its constituent parts, and to arrange those parts schematically, so as to show patterns of meaning. It is a useful, indeed essential means of making sense of the ideas in a novel, but the whole of a novel is more than its parts, and the analytic process, by dwelling on the parts, is unfair to the whole. At any rate, it does not take into account the effect of the whole, which is, properly speaking, what the experience of the novel involves.

In the case of *Passion Play* I am being especially unfair to the novel if I do not at least mention that it is, in the reader's experience of it, not a ruthless combatting of wills, a harsh system of shifting philosophical coordinates. It is a very moving love story. Vanessa is indeed possessive; she does indeed—perhaps scarcely realizing it herself—want to hold Fabian in ways probably destructive to him. As more than a teacher, as virtually a father to her, he has set her off in life, and his part is now to withdraw from her youth, and let her make her own life. But he loves her and she loves him. That much the reader feels, and their parting, however necessary, is not less sad for that reason.

Other aspects of the reader's experience of the novel should be mentioned. The accounts of the competitions, in polo or show jumping, are brilliantly written, clear to follow, full of tension. The sexual combats or competitions, which alternate with the athletic, complement and extend them, as I hope I have indicated. In *Passion Play*, in addition to the playful humor, and the almost complete elimination of the revenge theme, another new element is a movement towards a lusher use of language. Sometimes it is effective, but often it is a bit overblown. The novel also is divided into fewer passages or episodes, which in turn are more fully worked out and longer lasting than in the earlier novels; and, as in *Blind Date,* the movement toward a more conventional plot is apparent.

Fabian, Don Quixote, Captain Ahab, and Jerzy Kosinski

The epigraphs to *Passion Play* are from *Don Quixote* and *Moby Dick,* and throughout the novel connections are made between Fabian, Don Quixote, and Captain Ahab. Quixote and Ahab are both doomed madmen on hopeless quests to eliminate evil from the world. Both are in some ways pathetic, in some ways destructive, but finally noble and impressive, if for no other reason than because of their single-mindedness and sheer endurance.

As a Don Quixote-like character, Fabian, growing gaunt and old, is often described to us as carrying a "lance." Vanessa is called his "Dulcinea" (180), and in one of his riding stunts we see him riding up to Vanessa on a white horse, dressed in white, and throwing her a rose—before falling off the horse. The very last image of him in the book is of "a man on a horse, streaming along the black strip of runway, the man's helmet, shirt and breeches all white, his horse black, the run of the horse unbroken, the rider tilting, as if charging with a lance, in combat with an enemy only he could see" (271).

Fabian sometimes refers to himself, not only as a "Don Quixote of the turnpike," but also as a "Captain Ahab, moorless in his big ship of a VanHome" (72). He is perhaps most Ahab-like in that, as Ahab tended to see the entire world in the form of a whale, Fabian sees it in terms of the horse.

The other character, however, Fabian is most often parallelled with is Kosinski himself. Kosinski has called Fabian "my most perfect autobiographical character." "Polo is an allegory of my fiction." Kosinski points out to us that, like serious creative writing, polo is a marginal, small-audience game. There are 3,000 poets in the United States, and 3,000 polo players. Yet he feels it is a quintessential American sport, based on organized team violence, yet offering ample scope for the one-on-one individual star, who is a sort of refined version of the American cowboy.[6]

Even without Kosinski's help, we would see the many connections between him and Fabian. Fabian is foreign-born. He is a widower after his wife of five years died of cancer. Driving his VanHome is equated with the experience of reading a novel. His books on "equitation" obviously parallel his novels. For instance, his second book, *Obstacles,* the "audacity of its technique widely acclaimed," was awarded "the prestigious National Horse Lovers Award" (178), clearly points to *Steps* winning the National Book Award. The chair to his writing desk is made out of a saddle, thus underlining the connection between "writing" and "riding." A number of brief scenes—as in most Kosinski novels—recount actual occurrences in Kosinski's life.

Fabian's books, we learn, are not selling, the vogue for him increasingly fading. "'Down here they don't buy your books,' Stella said. 'They complain there are no pictures, not even drawings. And they get upset by what you write about riding'" (176). He distrusts pictures (and this is Kosinski's old argument against television) because "an excessive appeal to the sense of sight was insidious and debilitating, a specious claim to the reproduction of the world as it really was. He resisted the lulling implication that knowledge was above all what was to be seen, and refused the passive luxury of the spectator's chair, the flattening of reality. . . . He suspected that to submit to that vison would be to clog the active play of images that were fluent and mobile within each person, fantasy and emotion that written language alone could quicken" (178).

His appeal can never be to the mass television audience. Rather he is writing to the individual, one-on-one, but as the epigraph from *Don Quixote* insists, "It is only right, then, for every prince to think more highly of this last, or rather of this first species of knight errant. For, as we read in their histories, there have been some amongst them who have been the salvation, not only of one kingdom but of many."

Chapter Nine
The Stature of Jerzy Kosinski

Jerzy Kosinski has often spoken of his novels as constituting a "cycle," united by the common theme of the individual versus the society. Studied carefully in order, as we have just done in the preceding chapters, they seem like more than a cycle. They seem like the body and soul and lifetime of a twentieth-century man, Jerzy Kosinski. We see the child abandoned in wartime, an experience so alienating he refused to speak for several years. We see the savagely egoistical, manipulative, equally desperate life of the young manhood of a "survivor." And we watch him grow into at least a slightly mellowing middle age, the clear vision of impending mortality somehow salving the desperation, as he begins to work out a philosophy of "being" that can risk death for the sake of life, that can venture even its precious individuality for the possibility of love.

I made a brash statement in the Preface to this book. I said that Kosinski "is a major writer of international stature, a philosophical writer in the tradition of Sartre and Camus—except a much better and more original novelist than either of these." I have certainly failed in my endeavors if I have not, in these chapters, demonstrated over and over again the complex and original artistry of the novels, and the firm philosophical framework sustaining them. But more than that is needed to make a creative work major. We feel it should touch our experience centrally, and the charge is often made that Kosinski's characters and situations are marginal and exaggerated. Kosinski would reply that we are being naive, that violence and disarray are the experience of many and the expectation of most: "It depends, I think, primarily on your outlook. If you look upon the incidents in *The Painted Bird* and *Steps* and *Being There* as peripheral and insane and not too common, then you are bound to have a shock almost every day; but if you will see yourself as part of the larger community, if you will not

154

keep yourself in a locked compartment marked 'for sane only,' then you won't be very surprised when confronted by murder, persecution, or old age. Perhaps such an attitude would make you 'less sensitive'—but, conversely, that would mean that the least aware, the most provincial among us, is also the most sensitive."[1]

Kosinski's writing is aimed directly at eliminating our provincial "sensitivity." The longer we blandly assume that death and pain is the experience of the other guy, the marginal image on television, but no part of our own lives, the less we will be able to cope with those things when they do enter our lives. The more likely we will be to give up our independence to some "big brother," who will claim to spare us from the inevitable experiences of all living things. And finally, trusting in our safety and immortality, the more precious days we will waste, not realizing every non-repeatable moment should have the last grain of life extracted from it.

Of all Kosinski's works, *The Painted Bird* is, in my estimation, so far the best. It seems to be one of those inevitable conceptions, like *Huckleberry Finn* or *Robinson Crusoe* or *Wuthering Heights,* that, once experienced by the reader, can never again be quite forgotten, one of those magical novels in which myth, symbol, and reality effortlessly merge. It is the childhood of all of us, blotted out, or barely remembered in nightmare, or recalled in a children's fairytale, the tiny manling in a society of all-powerful giants whose speech and motives both are barely comprehensible.

Kosinski, I think, might find a lasting place in our literature on the basis of that one book. But I hope I have made clear in my book that he is not resting on that single success. It was no "sport," no fortuitous accident, no simple record of a life that by coincidence touched our lives as well. Kosinski has gone steadily onward, shaping his career as a serious novelist of the highest powers. I would like to point particularly to the three novels, *Cockpit, Blind Date,* and *Passion Play,* that may have been less popular, less enthusiastically received by the reviewers than some of the earlier novels, but which I believe (and I hope my chapters on these novels support my belief) serious readers and critics will pay increasing attention to, as they understand more and more what Kosinski is about.

I should not omit saying that, as a stylistic innovator, Kosinski has not left the form of the novel the way he found it. His experiments have been particularly interesting and fruitful in three directions. First, with his brief, achronological vignettes he has helped further to dislocate the structure of the traditional realistic novel of the nineteenth century, forcing the reader to give more attention to the event before his eye and less to the unfolding of some future dimension of the plot. Second, as I have tried to chart in my discussion of his novels, he has attempted in several ways to invade the world of his novels with quotations from "real" life, often, as in *Blind Date,* creating extremely powerful scenes from the tension between fact and fiction. Both these are kinds of experiments novelists have long been engaged in. He has furthered these experiments, and given them his personal stamp. Third, his very most interesting innovations have been in the treatment of his characters. He has given us protagonists easy to identify with and then has given these protagonists actions to perform that we draw back from, yet find ourselves implicated in. To a more extreme degree than any writer I know, Kosinski refuses to give us any moral guidelines, refuses to tell us which actions we should approve, which we should not. It is by design, because he intends to awaken us to making free moral decisions.

A moment ago I quoted a statement I had made in the Preface to the present book. In concluding my study I would like to quote myself once more, this time from the concluding lines of my discussion of *Blind Date:* "He has written several novels to point out the dangers and difficulties of life, but having personally been through many of the most traumatic upheavals and disruptions of our recent desperate history, he is in all senses a survivor. He has come through, and he has triumphed. More than most others, he is in a position to be an example to us."[2]

Notes and References

Chapter One

1. Clare D. Kinsman, ed., *Contemporary Authors: A Biobibliographical Guide to Current Authors and their Works,* Vols. 17–20, first revision (Detroit: Gale Research Co., 1976), p. 417. The motto comes from Descartes.

2. Shakespeare, *The Tempest,* I: ii.

3. Jerzy Kosinski, *The Painted Bird* (New York, 1966), p. 44.

4. On the book jacket of his third novel, *Being There,* he had the publisher make the "Z" in Jerzy bigger than any of the other letters on the jacket. This anecdote is told in Cleveland Amory, "Trade Winds," *Saturday Review,* April 17, 1971, p. 16.

5. Ibid.

6. Kosinski is of Jewish ancestry, according to *Current Biography Yearbook, 1974,* ed. Charles Moritz (New York: The H. W. Wilson Co., 1974), p. 212.

7. He barely understood the Ruthenian dialect of the peasants, to begin with. *Current Biography Yearbook,* p. 212; Wayne Warga, "Jerzy Kosinski Reaches Down into Life and Writes," *Los Angeles Times,* April 22, 1973, p. 1.

8. Warga, p. 54.

9. *Current Biography Yearbook,* p. 212.

10. Warga, p. 54.

11. George Plimpton and Rocco Landesman, "The Art of Fiction: Jerzy Kosinski," *Paris Review,* no. 54 (Summer 1972), p. 185 (henceforth identified as "Plimpton"); also, expanded in *Writers at Work,* ed. George Plimpton, (New York: Penguin Books, 1981), pp. 315–38.

12. Plimpton, p. 186; Jerome Klinkowitz, "Jerzy Kosinski," in *The New Fiction: Interviews with Innovative American Writers,* ed., Joe David Bellamy, (Urbana, Ill., 1974), p. 146.

13. Plimpton, p. 186.

14. Warga, p. 54. My account in the last two paragraphs is taken almost word for word from this source. The story of the invented patrons is told by Kosinski in Klinkowitz, p. 147.

15. Most accounts of his life say he knew no English, but Kosinski tells me he had enough knowledge of English sociological jargon to pick his way through professional journals.

16. When asked when he had really gained facility with English, he said, "In terms of writing, I would think about nine months after I arrived, but this has been a never-ending process. In terms of speaking, about a year and a half later, but I am still working at it." Klinkowitz, pp. 151–52.

17. The previous paragraphs are based on Warga, p. 54. Kosinski tells me as well as Ami Shinitzky, editor of *Polo Magazine, Equus,* and *Centaur,* how he grew up riding horses, as they were the backbone of agriculture and transportation in rural Eastern Poland. It was during his marriage with Mary Weir that he took up show jumping and polo; see also Kosinski's own autobiographical account in "Kosinski's Horses," an interview with Ami Shinitzky, in *Centaur,* no. 1 (Summer 1981).

18. Susanne McGanney, "Interview," *The Literary Guild Magazine,* February 1978, p. 3.

19. Warga, p. 54.

20. McGanney, p. 3.

21. *Current Biography Yearbook,* p. 212.

22. Plimpton, p. 189.

23. *Notes of the Author on "The Painted Bird,"* (New York, 1965), p. 9.

24. Amory, pp. 16–17.

25. Plimpton, p. 196.

26. Ibid.

27. *Current Biography Yearbook,* p. 213.

28. Plimpton, pp. 193–94.

29. Ibid., p. 183.

30. Georges Bratschi, "Rencontre Avec un Oiseau Bariolé," *Tribune de Genève,* May 8–9, 1976, p. 31.

31. *Current Biography Yearbook,* p. 213.

32. "The Psychological Novelist as Portable Man," *Psychology Today,* December 1977, p. 56.

33. Bratschi, p. 31.

34. Plimpton, p. 206. Following quotations in this section from this source in text identified by *PR.*

35. *Psychology Today,* December 1977, p. 55.

36. *Current Biography Yearbook,* p. 215.

37. Plimpton, p. 184.

38. Amory, p. 17.

39. *Psychology Today,* December 1977, p. 52. For a description of how the comet is used, see Chapter 3 below.

40. All quotations from Plimpton, pp. 195, 194.

41. Thomas Teicholz, "Happy, Busy and at War: A Profile of Jerzy Kosinski," Unpublished Master's Project, Columbia University School of Journalism, January 1980, p. 4.

42. Ibid., p. 23. Kosinski's working and social life is also a subject of *Social Stamina,* a profile of him and others by Marie Brenner, in *New York Magazine* (June 22, 1981).

Chapter Two

1. Jerzy Kosinski, *The Future Is Ours, Comrade* (pseud.: Joseph Novak) (Garden City, 1960). Parenthetical page numbers in the text are to this edition.
2. Daniel J. Cahill, in "Jerzy Kosinski: Retreat From Violence," *Twentieth Century Literature* 18 (April 1972): 122, briefly suggests that Kosinski's pose of neutrality in these books and his position as recording center, quite naturally moved into his imaginative fiction.
3. *Psychology Today,* December 1977, p. 55.
4. Perhaps this is not so surprising: Kosinski tells me he was already working on *Steps* and *The Painted Bird* at the same time he was writing *No Third Path.*
5. Jerzy Kosinski, *No Third Path* (pseud.: Joseph Novak) (Garden City, 1962), pp. 69–70 and passim. Parenthetical page numbers in the text are to this edition. Kosinski tells me it is the very same man and that it was through Gavrila's influence and position that many of his interviews and most of his Soviet research could take place.
6. Klinkowitz, p. 149.
7. "The reason for a difference in structure is that *The Future* was set to 'present' the attitudes, while *No Third Path* was to 'explain' the mechanics by carefully selected 'evidence.' The first was more 'open ended' (like *Steps*), the other 'centrifugal' (like *Cockpit*)," Kosinski told me in a telephone conversation.
8. In *Steps* (67–70) the character who hides in the lavatories is made almost a hero. At first, as an excuse for spending so much time in the lavatories, he carried a jar of cleaning fluid and erased antirevolutionary slogans scribbled in the stalls. "All of those erasures are a small price to pay" (69) for the peace and freedom from surveillance, he tells the protagonist. But later this same man openly defies the authorities, then commits suicide in one of the stalls. Suicide, for Kosinski, can be a positive act, affirming man's dignity by giving him control over natural process. See Chapter 4, below.

Chapter Three

1. Warga, p. 54.
2. Bratschi, p. 31.
3. Ibid.

4. Plimpton, p. 203.

5. Jerzy Kosinski, *The Painted Bird* (New York, 1966). Parenthetical page numbers in the text are to this edition. This edition is the first to have Kosinski's full, unaltered text. For Kosinski's problems with the first edition, see Klinkowitz, pp. 144–45.

6. Plimpton, p. 189.

7. Amory, p. 16.

8. *Current Biography Yearbook,* p. 212.

9. Warga, p. 54.

10. In *No Third Path*—see Chapter 2 above—Kosinski writes of a Gavrila who "had known me since the war and for a time—when I was alone—had been like a second father to me" (70).

11. In an interview, Kosinski stated, "I was mute for a longer time than was the Boy in *The Painted Bird*. He's mute for about three years, from 1942, let's say, to the end of 1945, when he regains his speech. I was mute from 1942 until 1948, more than six years" (Klinkowitz, p. 144).

12. *Current Biography Yearbook,* p. 212.

13. *Psychology Today,* December 1977, p. 128.

14. Ibid., p. 126.

15. Kosinski tells me that he is not quiet: he "has written *The Painted Bird*. It is about the war. War traumatizes: survival often reeks of corpses. So does the survival in *The Painted Bird*. . . and of the painted bird."

16. Kosinski tells us that he actually spared us some of the worst—perhaps when he cut the novel down by "a third."

17. There is a scene in the novel where the protagonist muses, "How many times had I dreamed of the time when I would be strong enough to return . . . [and] poison their children" (137). It is perhaps instructive to contrast this with a scene in *Steps* (34–37) that appears to be a scene which might have been considered for inclusion in *The Painted Bird,* in which the young boy actually does poison the children in the village.

18. *Psychology Today,* December 1977, p. 126.

19. Klinkowitz, p. 149.

20. Richard Byornson, *The Picaresque Hero in European Fiction* (Madison: University of Wisconsin Press, 1977), p. 17ff.

21. "Happy men," Kosinski has said, "don't waste their time beating and punishing others." *Psychology Today,* December 1977, p. 56.

22. *No Third Path,* p. 53.

23. Amory, p. 16.

24. Gail Sheehy:"It would seem that if you were to create your own world, you would want to give the individual the greatest amount of power of will and of freedom and reduce the power of the state, the restraints of

collectivity. Yet, many people want the various protections that society offers; so they often submit to restraints and relinquish many freedoms in exchange for such a collective protection." Kosinski: "This collective protection does not remove the threat of chance. . . . To me, such a promise is a lie. The institutions of society are objectively there, no doubt, but in terms of our private drama, they are nothing but a backdrop. We play our drama by ourselves, and when we finally exit, our play has come to an end." *Psychology Today,* December 1977, p. 55.

25. Ibid., p. 52. Kosinski, a little embarrassed, I think, by this passage, reminds me that he travels a great deal by car, often driving across hundreds of miles of empty space, and has to consider what would happen in the event of engine failure, feeling he can only count so much on the assistance of his nine-year-old Buick Electra convertible!

26. Ibid., p. 52.

27. Bratschi, p. 31.

28. "I am 44 now, and I don't recall one single moment in my life when I saw myself as a victim chosen by fate, even though I remembered being beaten, molested, ridiculed, punished, pushed around. I remember bleeding and vomiting and crying and suffering a lot of pain and looking for God to help me out, but what I remember above all is that in the midst of my misery, I kept seeing myself as merely one of a majority of people who suffered and were not happy—my oppressors included" (*Psychology Today,* December 1977, p. 56).

29. Other critics have commented on *The Painted Bird* as an "education" novel, though their details and focus have not been identical to mine. The idea is most fully worked out in David H. Richter, "The Three Denouements of Jerzy Kosinski's *The Painted Bird,*" *Contemporary Literature* 15 (Summer 1974): 373–76. The *Bildungsroman* idea is also touched on in Stanley Corngold, "Jerzy Kosinski's *The Painted Bird:* Language Lost and Regained," *Mosaic* 4 (Summer 1973): 165, and in Ivan Sanders, "The Gifts of Strangeness: Alienation and Creation in Jerzy Kosinski's Fiction," *Polish Review* 19 (1974): 173–75.

30. *Current Biography Yearbook,* p. 213.

31. In the essay itself Kosinski reminds us that "after the book is presented to the public, the writer becomes one of many readers of his own work, and his judgment of this work is yet another subjective judgment, neither more astute nor more shallow than the judgment of any other reader." *Notes of the Author on "The Painted Bird,"* p. 10. Parenthetical page numbers are to this edition. Kosinski's warning here is often forgotten by his critics, who in writing about *The Painted Bird* or *Steps,* often, in their discussions, quote his essays on those novels more often than they quote the

novels themselves. The danger, as Kosinski points out, is that the novelist himself may be a particularly poor critic of his work, since, knowing so well his *intention* when writing his novel, he may be blinded to what he has *actually* written.

32. Kosinski once remarked to me, "If a writer can invent a character who has never lived, why can't he invent for his fictions real-life living characters, himself for instance?"

33. "Natural symbolism presupposes the omnipotence of nature and is a throwback to a primitive period when men existed in a more direct relationship with nature" (Kosinski, *The Art of the Self*, p. 39).

34. This is also the position of Corngold, p. 161.

Chapter Four

1. See also Brandon Tartikoff, "Jerzy Kosinski," *Metropolitan Review*, October 8, 1971, p. 2.

2. Chuck Ross, "Rejected," *New West*, February 12, 1979, pp. 39ff.

3. I mean, we cannot demonstrate this simply by reading the book. Kosinski himself, however, has frequently informed us that there is indeed a single protagonist throughout. See note 15 below.

4. I: 3, 12, 13, 17; II: 3, 4, 5, 6,; III: 7, 8; IV: 1, 2, 3, 4, 5, 9; V: 2.

5. I: 10, 12, 13; II: 6; III: 5, 7; IV: 3(?).

6. For instance, a young girl coupling with a large farm animal, or, the protagonist making love long distance with a woman dying of consumption. The episodes are I: 1, 2, 3, 4, 5, 14, 17, 19; II: 4, 5, 6; III: 2, 4, 5; V: 2.

7. Jerzy Kosinski, *Steps* (New York, 1968). Parenthetical page numbers in the text are to this edition.

8. In terms of his philosophical intentions Kosinski would probably say that in living a lie for the sake of others' opinions of him, he has made of himself an object, and his "self," no longer subject to his own dictates, is at the mercy of others.

9. But see Kosinski's quite different interpretation of this scene in *The Art of the Self*, pp. 33–34: "The treatment by the villagers of the woman in the cage is the communal acting out of an obsession. To primitive people, feelings and obsessions—of anguish and fear—can be personified and acted out on a social level in dances, ritual, religion. . . . It is ironic that the woman is unbaptized and thus excluded from the Church. It is ironic, because the priest is obviously confronted here with something older than Catholicism."

10. *Psychology Today*, December 1977, p. 55.

11. *Current Biography Yearbook*, p. 214. See also Tartikoff, p. 2.

12. Plimpton, pp. 206–207.

13. Kosinski himself considered the language of *Steps* to be "closest to what I really wanted to do with English. The vision demanded a clear language, a language detached as the persons of the novel." Plimpton, pp. 196–97.

14. Jerzy Kosinski, *The Art of the Self* (New York, 1968). Parenthetical page numbers in the text are to this edition.

15. One critic (Robert Boyers, "Language and Reality in Kosinski's *Steps,*" *Centennial Review* 16 [Winter 1972]:44) uses the variety of characters as a demonstration that the novel cannot possibly have only a single protagonist. Kosinski has said "some critics saw in *Steps* several different male protagonists—as if afraid to recognize that our lives are not based on a single plot" (Klinkowitz, p. 163).

16. But most often Kosinski, as would be expected of a creative artist, speaks positively of the imagination "as a force which illuminates the meaning of our lives" (Klinkowitz, p. 162).

Chapter Five

1. Jerzy Kosinski, *Being There* (New York, 1970). Parenthetical page numbers in the text are to this edition.

2. Sanders, p. 180, sees a new theology centered around television as God and Creator.

3. Kosinski suggests that Stalin, Hitler, and Mao were just such technologically trumped-up images. See Bratschi, p. 31.

4. Amory, p. 16. But see Sanders, p. 116, for a number of interesting parallels between Chance and Kosinski. Also see note 16.

5. "Critics . . . were willing to accept 'Painted Bird' and 'Steps' as a reality of my life, but not money and industry. If anything, 'Being There' and 'Devil Tree' are more autobiographical than my other books. I consider 'Devil Tree' my private joke on American critics" (Warga, p. 54).

6. While in broad outlines the characters obviously resemble Weir and his wife, there is at least one very specific detail in common: Rand—the industrialist's name in *Being There*—has himself made up (50) before meeting the President, so the President will not realize quite how ill he actually is. The dying Weir did the same thing before board meetings.

7. As Kosinski himself points out in Bratschi, p. 31, and also in Daniel J. Cahill, *"The Devil Tree:* An Interview with Jerzy Kosinski," *North American Review,* Spring 1973, p. 57. The name Whalen is almost an amalgam of Yale and Wesleyan. Chance and the Old Man also, apparently, have real-life analogues. See Robert Hairman and Barbara Bottner, "Being There with Jerzy Kosinski," *L. A. Weekly* January 25–31, 1980, p. 7.

8. Jerzy Kosinski, *The Devil Tree* (New York, 1973). Parenthetical page numbers in the text are to this edition. Later in the chapter I also discuss the revised and expanded 1981 edition.

9. Kosinski, on the other hand, feels *The Devil Tree* is much closer to *The Painted Bird* than it is to either *Steps* or *Being There*. See Cahill, p. 56. See particularly his discussion of the differences in the use of the episodes in *Steps* and in *The Devil Tree* (Cahill, pp. 57–58).

10. I read as death-wish the passage—immediately after the passage where Whalen discusses Tibetan theories of life after death—where he crouches in the forest during a storm and listens to grasshoppers chirping: "The sound fascinated him. He had found the one calm place in the midst of the storm, a quiet voice calling him to the earth" (158); and as death-fear, the passage where he revisits the stretch of river where he and a friend were almost drowned under the ice (160–62)—a special trauma, we know, for Kosinski himself, who has claimed that the incident in *The Painted Bird* where the boy is almost drowned under the ice, and which terrified him of water ever after, was autobiographical (*Psychology Today,* December 1977, p. 126).

11. As further warning that we should study the novel itself and not pay too much attention to the novelist, in the Cahill interview, published five years after *The Art of the Self,* Kosinski now claims that language and the imagination—because they make communication possible—are the very things needed, the lack of which are destroying Whalen (Cahill, pp. 60–61).

12. If I am tentative in my discussion, I am in good company. Kosinski himself has said, "I feel that *The Devil Tree,* in terms of my old relation to my work, did something which puzzled me; I'm far more perplexed by *The Devil Tree* and by Jonathan and his environment, than by anything I have ever done in the past" (Cahill, p. 65).

13. Kosinski: "I guess the world has not been created as my water bed. . . . I was traumatized by water many times" (*Psychology Today,* December 1977, p. 126). In Cahill (p. 58), Kosinski hints that: "the last parts are in the third person; he may be dead by now." Later in that interview (p. 66) he gives other possible endings to the novel—but I think he is being evasive, unwilling to interpret the novel too directly for the reader.

14. *Psychology Today,* December 1977, p. 52.

15. Sanders, 178–79.

16. He in fact is a direct contrast to the boy in *The Painted Bird.* Both start from a position of childlike innocence, but the boy gains experience fast and is shaped by it. Chance remains totally unchanged. Kosinski has pointed out to me, however, certain other ways in which Chance can be considered autobiographical: "In the world of Mary Weir, in the world of steel, finance

and big business, Kosinski was a creature from another world to which *they* had no access. In fact, he came (was sent?) from a primitive garden of War-torn Europe *they* had seen only on television (a representation of it, to be sure, seldom if ever a documentary even). Thus, *they* had to assume things about Kosinski pretty much the way those around Chance assume they have access to what he thinks, to what he is."

17. Cahill, p. 56. Kosinski suggests to me that "Whalen might be K's prototypic *reader*—i.e. an archetypical 'addressee' of K's fiction, the very mind (American, Protestant, free to experience life and himself) K's fiction aims at. So," he goes on, "seem to be all other characters in *The Devil Tree.*" If other characters in Kosinski's novels are extensions of Kosinski or his environment, "Whalen is 'his own event'—who doesn't know how to become his own event. He has to be maintained (no comets here, oh no!) to 'live on interest.'"

Chapter Six

1. E.g., in Bratschi, p. 31.

2. Jerzy Kosinski, *Cockpit* (Boston, 1975). Parenthetical page numbers in the text are to this edition.

3. The episode follows closely Kosinski's own carefully engineered escape from Communist Poland. See Klinkowitz, p. 147.

4. *Psychology Today,* December 1977, p. 55.

5. I discussed Tarden's childhood acts of violence against others. Each of these actions might be considered as acts of revenge. Before he stabbed his Swiss nanny, an earlier nanny had used mildly traumatic means to stop him from crawling into her bed at night. The child he injured by dropping a heavy flowerpot near it had earlier broken one of his favorite toys. Most interesting is the episode where he phones people at random, telling them they had to go into the capital for a housing permit. Earlier his father had actually been called in for such a permit, which said that if he agreed to give up his former home, he could then live permanently in his present apartment. He had always talked about returning to his original home as soon as the disruptions of war were over, but now the young Tarden is surprised and disappointed to hear his father say he is happy that, with the new permit, he will not be forced to move again.

Is it partly contempt for his father for giving in to the regime that leads him to his cruel actions? When one of the men he calls excuses his own craven behavior by saying it is his destiny, the youthful Tarden sternly replies: "Destiny belonged to men, not men to destiny" (115).

6. In one episode, Tarden rents an old estate on two thousand acres next to the sea. When noisy night-time picnickers and lovers annoy him, he fills the area with electronic devices, and when people come the next night, he frightens them off by exploding charges, or playing recorded voices of Indian chants. Later, when a number of children trespass, he makes them believe they have murdered an Indian, takes several pictures of them, frightens them with the thought of long jail sentences, and lets them go. The townspeople, parents of the children, find out that he has concealed this crime of their children. Later he pretends that he has murdered two lesbians and buried them on the property, but the townspeople are afraid to prosecute for fear an investigation would also uncover the dead Indian. The scheme takes enormous effort and ingenuity on Tarden's part, but is not, properly speaking, a revenge scheme. He seems to have done it all for a prank.

7. Kosinski tells us this actually happened to him shortly after his first arrival in New York (Bratschi, p. 31).

8. The image is reminiscent of the animals he and other children drowned and froze into the ice in his childhood in a ritual of winter (119–20).

9. Bratschi, p. 31.

10. Geoffrey Movius, "A Conversation with Jerzy Kosinski," *New Boston Review* (Winter 1975):3.

11. Kosinski, who has often put characters in his novels who are, to a greater or lesser extent, like Mary Weir (the wife of the financier in *Being There*, Whalen's mother in *The Devil Tree*, Mary Kirkland in *Blind Date*), denies that he had any intention of making Theodora stand in any way for Mary Weir. But the parallels I have mentioned are there for the reader to judge. Writers are not always fully aware of their intentions.

12. If each way I choose to discuss the novel seems to result in a slightly different interpretation of it, I do not believe this calls my interpretations into question. Rather, it suggests that the novel is complex and multifaceted, and that a full experience of the novel demands that it be read on several, sometimes conflicting, levels at the same time.

Chapter Seven

1. Jerzy Kosinski, *Blind Date* (Boston, 1977). Parenthetical page numbers in the text are to this edition.

2. See Jacques Monod, *Chance and Necessity: An Essay on the Natural Philosophy of Modern Biology,* trans. Austryn Wainhouse (New York: Knopf, 1971), p. 114, for a similar chain of coincidences.

3. And certainly a central act of blind chance in the novel—though this one is verified by real life—occurs when Levanter is flying to visit his friends who are all gathered at Sharon Tate's house. There is a baggage mix-up on the planes, and Levanter, furious, is forced to hold up his trip for a day—and on the night he should have been at the Tate house, everyone there is murdered by the Manson gang.

4. Plimpton, p. 200. "Being there," of course, is a literal translation of *Dasein*.

5. I have taken my discussion from Marjorie Grene, "Martin Heidegger," in *The Encyclopedia of Philosophy*, ed. Paul Edwards (New York: Macmillan, 1967), III:459–65. Kosinski reminds me that Kierkegaard's *Either/Or* has also been a strong influence on him.

6. "I knew such a woman once [she is dead now]. . . . She was one of the most wholesome, most alive, beings I've met. Because of her joy of life, she was able to acquire and to convey a range of feelings, fantasies, and observations few of us have and all could benefit by." *Psychology Today*, December 1977, p. 55.

7. Ibid.

8. *Chance and Necessity*, pp. 172–73.

9. *Psychology Today*, December 1977, p. 55.

10. Perhaps Kosinski means to parallel the scene with that of the rape, where the girl's face cannot be seen.

11. *Psychology Today*, December 1977, p. 55.

12. *Encyclopedia of Philosophy*, III:463.

Chapter Eight

1. Jerzy Kosinski, *Passion Play* (New York, 1979). Parenthetical page numbers in the text are to this edition. At the time I am writing this book, no other edition is available. Kosinski tells me, however, that in the rush of publishing it, the book was printed from the wrong set of galley proofs, and that the 1980 Bantam edition will print the book as he intended it.

2. The scene can also be considered symbolically: the journalist, an old horseback rider with a very young bride, a rebel standing apart from the crowd, which is in collusion with the dictator, is rather like an elderly version of Fabian himself. When Fabian takes the journey into the uncharted interior of his psyche, what he discovers is that, drugged and controlled by the dictator, he is destroying himself, destroying his future. Falsalfa is doing it, but Fabian is letting him, which is why any court would find against him.

3. Her name is almost like his VanHome with a diminutive added, as if she were a kind of home for him.

4. Let me once more quote Kosinski's definition of love, "which, one supposes, is the attempt to be simultaneously subject and object, and is the willing relinquishment of the single subject to a new subject created from two single ones, each subject enhanced into one heightened self." *The Art of the Self,* p. 31.

5. In *Cockpit,* Tarden similarly offers to set up a trust fund for Valerie to make her independent, but she quickly realizes that "by appointing myself her liberator, I was actually prohibiting her from shaping her own existence; I was concerned only with my own future and had created an illusion of what I wanted her to be" (6).

6. On Milton Rosenburg's "Conversations from Chicago," on National Public Radio, October 8, 1979.

Chapter Nine

1. Plimpton, p. 191.

2. The problem with writing about an active living writer is that he does not sit still after you have tidily summed him up on your last page. Kosinski is already embarking on new ventures. Peter Sellers finally broke down Kosinski's resistance to having any of his novels made into film; and when the film of *Being There* (Kosinski's screenplay) appeared, Kosinski was so pleased that he is now willing to consider cinematic or theatrical adaptations of his other works, as well as writing an original story for film or theater. I predict further dazzling success for Kosinski, for what has he not succeeded at dazzlingly?

Selected Bibliography

PRIMARY SOURCES

1. Novels

Being There. New York: Harcourt Brace Jovanovich, 1971; New York: Bantam, 1974.

Blind Date. Boston: Houghton Mifflin, 1977; New York: Bantam, 1978.

Cockpit. Boston: Houghton Mifflin, 1975; New York: Bantam, 1976.

The Devil Tree. New York: Harcourt Brace Jovanovich, 1973; New York: Bantam, 1974. Revised and expanded edition, New York: St. Martin's Press, 1981; New York: Bantam, 1981.

The Painted Bird. Boston: Houghton Mifflin, 1965: revised edition with introduction by Kosinski, 1976; New York: Pocket Books, 1966; New York: Modern Library, 1970; New York: Bantam, 1972.

Passion Play. New York: St. Martin's Press, 1979; New York: Bantam, 1980.

Steps. New York: Random House, 1968; New York: Bantam, 1969.

2. Nonfiction Books

The Art of the Self: Essays à Propos "Steps." New York: Scientia-Factum, 1968.

The Future Is Ours, Comrade [pseud.: Joseph Novak]. Garden City, N.Y.: Doubleday, 1960.

Notes of the Author on "The Painted Bird." New York: Scientia-Factum, 1965.

No Third Path [pseud.: Joseph Novak]. Garden City, N.Y.: Doubleday, 1962.

3. Selected Articles

"Against Book Censorship." *Media & Methods,* January 1976, unpaged reprint.

"'The Banned Book' as Psychological Drug—a Parody." *Media & Methods,* January 1977, pp. 8–9.

"Dead Souls on Campus." *New York Times,* October 13, 1970, p. 20.

"The Disenchanted Pilgrim." *Time,* June 26, 1978, p. 22.

"The Lone Wolf." *American Scholar* 41 (Fall 1972):513–19.

"Our 'Predigested, Prepackaged Pop Culture'—a Novelist's View." *U.S. News & World Report,* January 8, 1979, pp. 52–53.

"Packaged Passion." *American Scholar* 42 (Spring 1973):193–204.

"The Reality Behind Words." *New York Times,* October 3, 1971, p. 23.

"To Hold a Pen." *American Scholar* 42 (Fall 1973):555–67.

4. Selected Interviews

Amory, Cleveland. "Trade Winds." *Saturday Review,* April 17, 1971, pp. 16–17.

Anon. "Painted Bird of Youth." *Guardian* [London], June 15, 1973, p. 10.

Blake, Jeanie. "Old Man River Lures Literary Giant to City." [New Orleans] *Times-Picayune,* October 21, 1979, p. 10.

Bratschi, Georges. "Rencontre Avec un Oiseau Bariolé: Kosinski: Sauter du 'Cockpit' pour Échapper à l'Agonie." *Tribune de Genève,* May 8–9, 1976, p. 31.

Cahill, Daniel J. *"The Devil Tree:* An Interview with Jerzy Kosinski." *North American Review,* Spring 1973, pp. 56–66.

———. "Life at a Gallop." *Washington Post,* September 16, 1979, p. 10.

———. "An Interview with Jerzy Kosinski on *Blind Date." Contemporary Literature* 19 (Spring 1978):133–42.

Christian, George. "A Passion for Polo." *Houston Chronicle,* October 7, 1979, pp. 18ff.

Collins, Nancy. "Jerzy Kosinski Is the Zbig of Books." *Washington Star,* February 10, 1980, pp. F1ff.

Cross, Linda. "Kosinski on Skiing." *Skiing,* November 1977, pp. 143ff.

Evans, Christopher. "Jerzy Kosinski: Passionate Player." *Minneapolis Star* (Saturday Magazine), September 22, 1979, pp. 8–11.

Gallo, William. "Jerzy Kosinski: Writing by Chance and Necessity." *Rocky Mountain News,* November 30, 1977, pp. 63ff.

Hairman, Robert, and Bottner, Barbara. "Being There with Jerzy Kosinski." *L.A. Weekly,* January 25–31, 1980, pp. 7ff.

Klinkowitz, Jerome. "Jerzy Kosinski: An Interview." In *The New Fiction: Interviews with Innovative American Writers.* Edited by Joe David Bellamy. Urbana: University of Illinois Press, 1974, pp. 142–68.

Lawson, Carol. "Jerzy Kosinski." *New York Times Book Review,* October 21, 1979, p. 58.

McGanney, Susanne. "Interview." *Literary Guild,* February 1978, p. 3.

Movius, Geoffrey. "A Conversation with Jerzy Kosinski." *New Boston Review,* 1 (Winter 1975):3–7.

Northouse, Cameron, and Northouse, Donna, "VanHome of the Mind." *Lone Star Book Review,* November 1979, pp. 6ff.

Nowicki, R. E. "An Interview with Jerzy Kosinski." *San Francisco Review of Books,* March 1978, pp. 10–13.

Plimpton, George, and Landesman, Rocco, "The Art of Fiction: Jerzy Kosinski." *Paris Review,* No. 54 (Summer 1972):183–207.

Sheehy, Gail. "The Psychological Novelist as Portable Man." *Psychology Today,* December 1977, pp. 54ff.

Silverman, Art. "The Renegade Novelist Whose Life is Stranger than Fiction." *Berkeley Barb,* November 25–December 1, 1977, pp. 8–9.

Sohn, David. "A Nation of Videots." *Media & Methods,* April 1975, pp. 24ff.

Sweeny, Louise. "Jerzy Kosinski and the Nine Million Dollar Glass of Water." *Christian Science Monitor,* March 1, 1979, pp. B4ff.

Tartikoff, Brandon. "Jerzy Kosinski." *Metropolitan Review,* October 8, 1971, p. 104.

Teicholz, Tom. "Being There and Staying There: Jerzy Kosinski." *Interview Magazine,* February 1980, pp. 34–35.

Walter, John. "The Anguish of Jerzy Kosinski and His Film." *Washington Post,* February 3, 1979, p. D–2.

Warga, Wayne. "Jerzy Kosinski Reaches Down into Life and Writes." *Los Angeles Times,* April 22, 1973, pp. 1ff.

SECONDARY SOURCES

Aldridge, John W. "The Fabrication of a Culture Hero." *Saturday Review,* April 24, 1971, pp. 25–27. Makes the important statement that Kosinski, not being an American, luckily does not have the American writer's fear of ideas. He is a philosophical writer in "the tradition of classic European modernism."

Boyers, Robert. "Language and Reality in Kosinski's *Steps.*" *Centennial Review* 16 (Winter 1972):41–61. Claims Irving Howe does not understand *Steps* very well, but actually takes us very little further into it himself. Boyers thinks there are several different protagonists in the novel and that the novel is not existential in its treatment of ideas— both of these ideas are refuted in this book.

Broyard, Anatole. "Casual Lust, Occasional Journalism." *New York Times Book Review,* November 6, 1977, p. 14. After totally failing to understand *Blind Date,* dismisses it as "lurid" and "pretentious."

Cahill, Daniel J. "Jerzy Kosinski: Retreat from Violence." *Twentieth Century Literature* 18 (April 1972): 121–32. Although *The Painted Bird* and *Steps* are both bleak and violent works, Cahill believes he sees aready in them a turning from violence toward something more hopeful.

Coale, Samuel. "The Quest for the Elusive Self: The Fiction of Jerzy Kosinski." *Critique* 15 (1973):25–37. Kosinski's characters search for themselves within the fragments of an impenetrable world. In *Being There,* the self finally vanishes and with it Kosinski's power as a writer. Coale hopes Kosinski can pull out of this void.

Corngold, Stanley. "Jerzy Kosinski's *The Painted Bird:* Language Lost and Regained." *Mosaic* 4 (Summer 1973):153–67. Sees the boy's becoming mute and then regaining his voice as the central image of the book. The recovered voice is the voice of art, our only bulwark against hatred and "the brute assault of the time that will engulf it."

Howe, Irving. "From the Other Side of the Moon." *Harper's Magazine,* March 1969, pp. 102–05. Feels that in *The Painted Bird,* the brutality is overdone. *Steps* is a better, more controlled work. He is convinced it has aesthetic and moral order in it, but confesses his inability to find out what that order is.

Hutchinson, James D. "Retrospect: Judging a Book Award." *Denver Quarterly* 4 (Autumn 1969):128–35. Feels *Steps* deserved the National Book Award for its universality. Says the novel is not to be interpreted but experienced.

———. "The 'Invisible Man' as Anti-Hero." *Denver Quarterly* 6 (Spring 1971):86–92. Slight essay comparing *Being There* and *Steps* that finds Chance in *Being There* to be a "TV-man."

Kanfer, Stefan. "When Going is the Goal." *Time,* September 17, 1979, p. 105. Negative review of *Passion Play.* Says the equestrian combats are masterful, but the sex scenes are out of Harold Robbins. "For the past several books, Kosinski has been as aimless as his characters."

Kennedy, William. "Kosinski's Hero Rides On." *Washington Post,* September 16, 1979. Intelligent review of *Passion Play;* sees the softer more human protagonist as a promising new direction for Kosinski, to keep him from the danger of self-parody if he just keeps repeating his former protagonists.

Klinkowitz, Jerome. "Insatiable Art and the Great American Quotidian." *Chicago Review* 25 (Summer 1973):174–77. Brief but sharp insights into *The Devil Tree.* Whalen tries to find himself and experience love, but is blocked by his past roots, from which he is unwilling to become independent.

———. "Jerzy Kosinski." In *Literary Disruptions: The Making of a Post-Contemporary American Fiction.* Urbana: University of Illinois Press, 1975, pp. 82–101, 218–21. The chapter on Kosinski mainly recapitulates Klinkowitz's interview with the author in *The New Fiction* (see "Selected Interviews," above). The book, however, includes a useful bibliography of Kosinski.

Lustig, Arnold. "Love and Death in New Jerzy." *Washington Post,* November 27, 1977, p. E1. Points out that Kosinski uses sex "as a fully or partly opened door to human nature, to human character. . . . Sex is the most reliable open door to the human soul."

Michelson, Peter. *"Blind Date." American Book Review* 1 (April-May 1978):5–7. This curious essay-review attacks *Blind Date* because in it Kosinski seems to be opposed to socialism and to favor capitalism.

Richter, David H. "The Three Denouements of Jerzy Kosinski's *The Painted Bird." Contemporary Literature* 15 (Summer 1974):370–85. Interesting discussion of the different endings to *The Painted Bird* as Kosinski revised it over the first three editions.

Sanders, Ivan. "The Gifts of Strangeness: Alienation and Creation in Jerzy Kosinski's Fiction." *Polish Review* 19 (1974):171–89. This most intelligent and insightful essay on Kosinski available discusses the first four novels, particularly the alienation—but great strength to endure—of the characters.

Shinitzky, Ami. "Life Is a Drama: Jerzy Kosinski: The Man and His Work." *Polo,* December 1979, pp. 21ff. A polo player's very literate discussion of *Passion Play* and how it relates to the game of polo.

Stone, Elizabeth. "Horatio Algers of the Nightmare." *Psychology Today,* December 1977, pp. 59–64. Because of the nightmare of their world, Kosinski characters numb themselves in various ways in order to survive. The risk is that in so doing, they will lose the very self they seek to preserve. Levanter in *Blind Date* is the first dimly hopeful character.

Swindell, Larry. "The Cruelest Game of Chance Is Life Itself." *Philadelphia Inquirer,* November 27, 1977, p. 12-H. A very intelligent reading of *Blind Date,* except for the conclusion that Levanter is "Kosinski's most pitiable character." Swindell is probably alone in thinking *The Devil Tree* Kosinski's best work.

Teicholz, Thomas. "Happy, Busy and at War." Columbia University Graduate School of Journalism Master's Project, January, 1980, 24 pages. This profile of Kosinski, based in part on interviews with Kosinski's friends, suggests that Kosinski's life is fairly regular, with most of his time given to writing.

Index

(The works of Kosinski are listed under his name)